the thatched kitchen™

HARVEST & HOLIDAY COOKBOOK

Book Trade Distribution by
DOUBLEDAY & COMPANY, INC.
Garden City, New York

TESTED RECIPE PUBLISHERS, INC. CHICAGO, ILLINOIS 60648 trp®

Library of Congress Catalog Card Number 72-87655
ISBN 0385 01757 X

Book design by Alice Harth
Photography by Elmer Moss
Photography on pages 21 and 59 by George de Gennaro
Recipes and text by Patricia Collier, Manager, Home Economics-Consumer Services,
    CASTLE & COOKE, INC., Foods Division

contents

the king of fruits and the fruit of kings

a symbol of hospitality

In the early 18th century, the Duchess of Marlborough served her guests a rare and exotic fruit—pineapple. Among the guests was famed poet James Thompson. He later recalled his delight with the taste in a book called Seasons:

The pride of vegetable life, beyond whate'er
The poet imaged in the Golden Age
Quick, let me strip thee of thy tufty coat,
Spread thy ambrosial stores and feast with Jove.

As far back as Charles II pineapple graced the tables only of royalty and the very wealthy. It was costly and rare and considered the "pinnacle of perfection" in flavor. The decorative pineapple motif was soon adopted in silver, crystal, china and fine furniture. It was even used in architecture over doorways and in formal gardens. In fact, the pineapple symbol was in evidence wherever guests were welcomed, sheltered, entertained or refreshed.

It is rumored that Christopher Columbus discovered pineapple on his journeys to the New World, but it was almost 150 years later that it found its true home in Hawaii, where the year-round sunny climate, tropical rains and rich volcanic soil, produced the world's finest pineapple.

In 1901 James D. Dole became the first successful pineapple packer in Hawaii, establishing what is now the world's largest fruit cannery. Today, whether it be fresh, frozen or canned, pineapple is still a symbol of hospitality especially if it bears the name Dole. Because it means you are serving your guests the best.

And what could be a better time for entertaining than the bountiful Fall season? We are sure you will find The Thatched Kitchen bountiful with ideas to express your hospitality.

Patricia Callier

CASTLE & COOKE, INC., Foods Division

appetizers

Seafood Cocktail Lanai

Serve this ever-popular cocktail in the living room for a nice change of pace.

1 can (1 lb., 4 oz.) Dole Pineapple Chunks
½ pound fresh cooked shrimp*
Seafood cocktail sauce
Lettuce
Chives

Drain pineapple. Toss chunks with shrimp and cocktail sauce to taste. Chill well. Spoon into lettuce-lined cocktail glasses and sprinkle with chives to serve. Makes 6 servings.
*Or use 2 cans (4 oz. each) shrimp, drained.

Zippy Appetizer Cheesecake

Cheesecake as an appetizer? Oh yes—when the crust is cheese cracker crumbs and the filling tangy with olives, onions and curry. Serve it in wedges in the living room as a surprise treat!

2 cups cheese cracker crumbs
6 tablespoons butter, melted
1 can (1 lb., 4 oz.) Dole Crushed Pineapple
1 envelope unflavored gelatin
2 tablespoons lemon juice
1 package (8 oz.) cream cheese, softened
1½ cups dairy sour cream
1 teaspoon salt
½ teaspoon curry powder
2 dashes tabasco
½ cup chopped pimiento-stuffed green olives
⅓ cup finely chopped celery
⅓ cup thinly sliced green onion

Combine cracker crumbs and butter; mix well. Set aside ¼ cup for top of cheesecake. Spread remainder over bottom of 9-inch spring form pan. Drain pineapple reserving ¼ cup syrup. Soften gelatin in reserved syrup and lemon juice. Dissolve over hot water. Cool to room temperature. Beat cream cheese until very soft. Gradually beat in gelatin. Blend in sour cream, salt, curry powder and tabasco. Fold in olives, celery, onion and well drained pineapple. Spoon into pan over cracker crumbs. Sprinkle reserved crumbs on top. Refrigerate overnight before cutting. Makes 10 to 12 servings.

Overleaf:
Seafood Cocktail Lanai

6

BLEU cheese dunk

Crisp raw vegetables or apple wedges are perfect "dunkers" for this snappy bleu cheese blend.

1 package (8 oz.) cream cheese, softened
1 package (4 oz.) bleu cheese, softened
2 tablespoons snipped chives
1 teaspoon dill weed
1 teaspoon seasoned salt
¼ teaspoon garlic powder
1 can (8¼ oz.) Dole Crushed Pineapple
Fresh raw vegetables

Beat together cream cheese and bleu cheese until fluffy. Beat in chives, dill weed, seasoned salt and garlic powder until blended. Fold in pineapple and all syrup. Chill 1 to 2 hours before serving with crisp vegetables. Makes 2 cups dip.

melt away crab bites

Bake these succulent morsels early in the day, then reheat a few minutes to crisp before serving.

Filling: 1 can (7½ oz.) Alaska King crabmeat
1 can (13¼ oz.) Dole Crushed Pineapple
½ cup finely chopped celery
¼ cup chopped green onions
2 tablespoons Dijon-style mustard
2 teaspoons garlic salt
2 teaspoons lemon juice

Crust: 1 package (11 oz.) pastry mix*
1 package (3 oz.) cream cheese, softened
1 egg yolk, slightly beaten

Drain crabmeat and pineapple well; combine with celery, onion, mustard, garlic salt, and lemon juice blending well.

Combine pastry mix and cream cheese, working with hands to form pastry dough. Roll out on a very well floured board to approximately ⅛-inch thickness. Cut into rounds with a 3-inch round cookie cutter. Spoon approximately 2 teaspoons of crabmeat filling into center of each pastry circle. Fold over and press edges with tines of a fork. Beat egg yolk slightly. Brush over crab pastries. Bake in a preheated 400°F. oven 10 to 15 minutes until golden. Serve warm. Makes approximately 3½ dozen.
*Mix for 2-crust pie.

chutney cheese pâté

Quick and easy to fix for drop-in guests. If you find there is too much topping, serve the extra in a small bowl alongside to be spooned over as needed.

1 package (8 oz.) cream cheese
1 can (1 lb., 4 oz.) Dole Crushed Pineapple
1 jar (8 oz.) chutney
Sesame crackers

Unwrap and place cream cheese in a block on a large wooden serving tray. Drain pineapple well. Combine with chutney until blended. Spoon over cream cheese. Surround with sesame crackers to serve. Makes approximately 35 servings.

chinese SPRING ROLLS

Baked instead of deep fat fried, these Oriental inspired appetizers capture the flavor without the fuss.

1 can (1 lb., 4 oz.) Dole Crushed Pineapple, drained
1 can (4 oz.) diced water chestnuts, drained
⅓ cup chopped green onions
1 can (1 lb.) bean sprouts, drained
2 cans (4 oz. ea.) deveined shrimp, drained,
   or ¾ lb. fresh cooked shrimp
2 cans (8 oz. ea.) refrigerated crescent rolls
Soy sauce

Combine pineapple, water chestnuts, onions and bean sprouts. Chop and fold in shrimp. Open one can refrigerated rolls. Unroll dough. Separate into 4 rectangles. Pinch diagonal separations together. Roll each rectangle on lightly floured board to 7 x 9-inches. Cut each rectangle into 3 strips 7 x 3-inches each. Spoon one heaping tablespoon filling into center of each strip, spreading lengthwise. Moisten edges with water. Roll dough over filling lengthwise. Press open ends with tines of a fork. Remove to lightly greased cookie sheet. Repeat with second can of rolls. Bake in preheated 375°F. oven for 15 to 20 minutes. Slice each diagonally into 3 bite-size rolls. Serve hot with soy sauce as dunk if desired. Makes 72 hors d'oeuvres.
Glaze: Brush with beaten whole egg if desired before baking.

harvest quiche

An elegant appetizer of French heritage—quiche is best served warm. If you bake it early, reheat just before serving.

Pastry: 1 cup sifted all-purpose flour
     ½ teaspoon salt
     ⅓ cup shortening
     2 to 3 tablespoons cold milk

Filling: 1 can (8¼ oz.) Dole Crushed Pineapple
     3 eggs
     1 cup light cream
     ¾ teaspoon salt
     1/16 teaspoon white pepper
     3 drops tabasco
     1½ cups grated Cheddar cheese
     6 slices cooked, crumbled bacon
     1 tablespoon chopped parsley

Combine flour and salt in a small bowl. Cut in shortening. Add milk to make a stiff dough. Shape into a ball. Roll on lightly floured board to a 12-inch circle. Fit into a 9-inch quiche pan, trimming so dough extends ⅛-inch above edge of pan. Set pan on cookie sheet. Bake in a preheated 425°F. oven 10 minutes. Meanwhile, prepare filling. Drain pineapple well. Beat eggs with cream, salt, pepper and tabasco. Stir in cheese and pineapple. Turn into partially baked pastry shell. Sprinkle with bacon and parsley. Return to hot oven and bake 20 minutes longer until set in center. Allow to stand 10 minutes before cutting. Makes 1 (9-inch) quiche.

Chinese Spring Rolls

JUGGED CHEDDAR SPREAD

Mellowed with a little port, this tangy cheddar spread is sure to please the men.

1 can (13¼ oz.) Dole Crushed Pineapple
1 package (8 oz.) cream cheese, softened
2 cups shredded Cheddar cheese
⅓ cup ruby port wine
1 tablespoon seasoned salt
½ teaspoon garlic powder
½ teaspoon hot dry mustard
2 tablespoons chopped parsley

Drain pineapple well. Beat softened cream cheese with cheddar and wine until smooth. Beat in seasoned salt, garlic powder and mustard. Fold in parsley and drained pineapple. Chill well before serving.* Makes 3 cups spread.
*Can be prepared a day in advance, covered and chilled overnight if desired.

ANTIPASTO NAPOLI

Gay Italian dinners always begin with an appetizer tray, be it simple or elaborate. Here's one you can make to capture the spirit.

1 can (7 oz.) tuna
1 can (1 lb.) cut green beans
1 can (15¼ oz.) kidney beans
1 can (1 lb., 4 oz.) Dole Pineapple Chunks
1 can (5¾ oz.) pitted ripe olives
1 jar (6 oz.) marinated artichoke hearts
¾ cup red wine vinegar
⅓ cup olive oil
1 tablespoon chopped parsley
1 tablespoon capers
1 tablespoon garlic salt
1 teaspoon oregano
1 teaspoon sweet basil
French bread

Turn tuna out into center of 2-inch deep serving platter. Drain green beans and kidney beans. Arrange on opposite sides of tuna. Drain pineapple reserving ⅓ cup syrup. Arrange pineapple between beans on one side. Drain and halve olives; arrange opposite pineapple to fill up platter. Drain artichoke marinade into reserved pineapple syrup. Sprinkle artichokes over tuna. Blend vinegar, olive oil, parsley, capers, garlic salt, oregano and sweet basil with reserved pineapple syrup. Pour over entire tuna platter. Cover with foil, marinate in refrigerator 2 to 3 hours. Serve with French bread as first course appetizer. Makes 6 to 8 servings.

SOUPS

danish fruit soup

Chilled fruit soup is a tradition in Denmark. It piques the appetite and doubles as salad when greens are scarce.

1 can (1 lb., 4 oz.) Dole Pineapple Chunks
1 can (1 lb.) pitted dark sweet cherries
1 can (11 oz.) mandarin oranges
¾ cup dry vermouth
2 tablespoons cornstarch
¼ cup water
1 teaspoon grated lemon peel
2 tablespoons fresh lemon juice
¼ teaspoon ground cardamom
¼ teaspoon ground coriander
1 cup dairy sour cream
Fresh mint sprigs

Drain pineapple, cherries, and mandarin oranges reserving all syrup. Combine fruit syrups, vermouth, cornstarch, water, lemon peel and juice, cardamom and coriander in a saucepan. Bring to a boil stirring constantly until mixture boils and thickens. Remove from heat. Stir in fruit. Chill 3 to 4 hours. Serve in crystal goblets or wine glasses, topped with a dollop of sour cream and mint sprig to garnish. Makes 6 to 8 servings.

mulligatawny soup

Hearty enough for a whole meal at home, it travels well in a thermos for snow bunny picnics, too.

4 slices bacon
¼ cup butter
1 cup diced onions
2 large carrots, diced
2 cups diagonally sliced celery
3 tablespoons flour
2 teaspoons curry powder
4 tablespoons chicken seasoned stock base*
1 quart water*
2 cups dry white wine
1 can (1 lb. 12 oz.) whole tomatoes
1 can (1 lb., 4 oz.) Dole Crushed Pineapple
¼ cup raw regular rice
1 teaspoon garlic salt
½ teaspoon thyme
2 cups chunked cooked chicken

Snip bacon into bite-size pieces. Sauté in a large heavy 6-quart saucepan until crisp. Remove with slotted spoon and reserve. Add butter to bacon drippings and sauté onions, carrots, and celery until onion is wilted. Stir in flour and curry powder until well blended. Add chicken stock base, water, wine, tomatoes, pineapple and all syrup and rice. Blend well. Stir in garlic salt and thyme. Cover and simmer 3 hours. Stir in chicken ½ hour before serving. Makes approximately 4 quarts.
*Or use 1 quart well-seasoned chicken stock in place of water and stock base.

11

senegalese soup

British inspired from their East Indian campaigns, this elegant cool and creamy soup has a subtle curry flavor.

2 tablespoons butter
2 teaspoons curry powder
2 tablespoons flour
2 cans (13¾ oz. ea.) chicken broth
1 can (8 oz.) coconut juice
1 can (13¼ oz.) Dole Crushed Pineapple
1 teaspoon seasoned salt
1 egg, beaten
½ cup whipping cream
Thin cucumber slices

Melt butter in a large saucepan. Blend in curry powder until foamy. Blend in flour. Stir in chicken broth and coconut juice. Drain pineapple well; stir in pineapple syrup and seasoned salt. Simmer 20 minutes for flavors to blend. Beat together egg and cream. Stir a little hot mixture into cream. Return to hot mixture, stirring constantly. Remove from heat. Stir in drained pineapple. Chill 2 to 3 hours in a covered glass bowl in refrigerator. Serve in small chilled soup cups, garnished with cucumber slices. Makes 8 servings.

fruited wine consommé

Sparkling, sophisticated and delicate of flavor, this soup is a perfect beginning for a very *special* dinner.

2 cans (10 oz. ea.) consommé
¼ cup chopped chutney
1 can (1 lb., 4 oz.) Dole Crushed Pineapple
1½ envelopes unflavored gelatin
¾ cup white dinner wine
½ teaspoon onion salt
1 teaspoon Worcestershire sauce
¼ cup fresh lemon juice
8 lemon slices for garnish
1 tablespoon chopped chives

Combine consommé, chutney and pineapple with all syrup in a large saucepan. Stir gelatin into wine to soften. Add to consommé. Stir in onion salt and Worcestershire sauce. Heat stirring constantly until mixture boils and gelatin dissolves. Remove from heat. Stir in lemon juice. Chill until firm. Spoon into 8 chilled icers. Top each with lemon slice and a sprinkle of chives. Makes 8 servings.

celestial soup

No waistline watching here. Real whipped cream is essential to the exciting subtle flavor.

2 cans (13¾ oz. ea.) chicken broth
1 can (8¼ oz.) Dole Crushed Pineapple
½ teaspoon grated lemon peel
¼ teaspoon seasoned salt
1 cup whipping cream
1 teaspoon curry powder
Snipped chives

Combine chicken broth, pineapple and all syrup, lemon peel and seasoned salt in a saucepan. Heat to boiling. Meanwhile, whip cream with curry powder until stiff. Pour soup into 6 small soup cups. Spoon cream over top. Garnish with snipped chives to serve. Makes 6 servings.

Overleaf:
Fruited Wine Consommé
Senegalese Soup
Mulligatawny Soup, *page 11*

salads

chutney chicken salad

Are the girls coming for lunch? This is an elegant salad to make ahead for gracious hostessing.

1 can (1 lb., 4 oz.) Dole Pineapple Chunks
2 tablespoons instant minced onions
2 cups diced cooked chicken
1 cup chunked cucumber
½ cup chopped salted cashews
1 cup mayonnaise
2 tablespoons chutney
1 teaspoon seasoned salt
Crisp lettuce leaves

Drain pineapple well reserving 3 tablespoons syrup. Combine minced onions and pineapple syrup, allowing mixture to stand 10 minutes until moisture is absorbed. Meanwhile combine chicken, cucumbers, cashews and pineapple chunks in a large bowl. Combine mayonnaise, chutney and seasoned salt. Add onions blending well. Pour over chicken mixture. Arrange lettuce leaves on 6 salad plates. Spoon chicken mixture onto lettuce. Makes 6 servings.

dilled salmon mousse

Crisp, crunchy vegetables provide a delightful textural quality to this delicate salmon mold.

2 cans (1 lb. ea.) salmon
¼ cup lemon juice
2 envelopes unflavored gelatin
1 cup dry white wine
½ cup mayonnaise
2 teaspoons prepared mustard
¾ teaspoon salt
¼ teaspoon dill weed
⅛ teaspoon white pepper
8 drops tabasco
1 can (8¼ oz.) Dole Crushed Pineapple
⅓ cup chopped celery
2 tablespoons chopped green onion
2 tablespoons chopped pimiento
1 cup whipping cream
Cucumber slices

Drain salmon reserving all liquid. Remove skin and large bones from salmon and flake fish. Combine ½ cup salmon liquid and lemon juice; sprinkle with gelatin. Let stand a few minutes to soften; set over hot water to dissolve. Stir in wine and cool. Add mayonnaise, mustard, salt, dill weed, pepper and tabasco; mix well. Drain pineapple well. Fold in flaked salmon and pineapple. Chill until mixture begins to thicken. Add vegetables. Whip cream until stiff. Fold into salmon mixture. Turn into oiled 6½-cup ring mold; chill firm. Unmold and garnish with cucumber slices. Makes 8 to 10 servings.

15

PICNIC PERFECT POTATO SALAD

Well chilled before you leave, this salad can be kept chilled in the beverage cooler until ready to serve.

1 quart chunked cooked pared potatoes
1 can (1 lb., 4 oz.) Dole Pineapple Chunks
4 slices bacon
½ cup chopped green onions
1 tablespoon flour
2 teaspoons seasoned salt
½ teaspoon celery seed
½ cup cider vinegar
½ cup sliced ripe olives
1 tablespoon chopped parsley

Turn potatoes into a deep bowl. Drain pineapple reserving ⅓ cup syrup. Add pineapple chunks to potatoes. Fry bacon crisp, remove with slotted spoon and drain on paper towels. Add onion to bacon fat and cook until wilted. Stir in flour, salt and celery seed. Blend in reserved pineapple syrup and cider vinegar until mixture thickens and boils. Pour over potatoes tossing well. Stir in olives and parsley. Chill well. Garnish with crumbled bacon to serve. Makes 4 to 6 servings.

SAVORY HAM SALAD

Turn left-over ham into a scrumptious supper salad.

1 can (1 lb., 4 oz.) Dole Pineapple Chunks
1 can (11 oz.) mandarin oranges
1 can (4 oz.) water chestnuts
2 cups cooked ham strips
½ cup chopped green onions
½ large cucumber (½ cup slices)
1 large avocado
½ cup mayonnaise
1 tablespoon red wine vinegar
1 teaspoon seasoned salt
½ teaspoon dill weed
Crisp salad greens

Drain pineapple well reserving two tablespoons of syrup. Drain mandarin oranges and water chestnuts. Combine with ham strips and green onions in a large bowl. Score cucumber with a fork; slice thinly. Peel and dice avocado, add to ham mixture. Blend mayonnaise, pineapple syrup, red wine vinegar, seasoned salt and dill weed. Pour over ham mixture, tossing lightly to combine. Spoon onto crisp salad greens to serve. Makes 6 servings.

COOL CUCUMBER SALAD

Piquant and light, it steals the show at early fall dinners.

1 package (6 oz.) lime gelatin
2 cups boiling water
1 can (1 lb., 4 oz.) Dole Crushed Pineapple
1 tablespoon vinegar
1½ teaspoons celery salt
½ teaspoon dill weed
1 cup dairy sour cream
1 cup grated cucumber, drained
Crisp salad greens

Dissolve gelatin in boiling water. Drain pineapple well to make 1 cup syrup. Add pineapple syrup, vinegar, celery salt and dill weed to gelatin. Chill until mixture reaches consistency of unbeaten egg white. Fold in sour cream, grated cucumber and pineapple. Pour into a 2-quart mold. Chill firm. Unmold onto crisp salad greens to serve. Makes 8 to 10 servings.

IMPERIAL CRAB SALAD

For sophisticated friends, or as a special family treat, this salad can be the focal point of the meal.

1 large head iceberg lettuce
1 can (1 lb., 4 oz.) Dole Sliced Pineapple
2 cans (7½ oz. ea.) Alaska King crabmeat
2 large avocados
⅓ cup red wine vinegar
¼ cup olive oil
1 tablespoon garlic salt
1 teaspoon dry mustard
½ teaspoon tarragon leaves, crumbled
1 tablespoon capers

Wash lettuce well; remove core but keep in tight head. Slice crosswise into 5 thick slices. Place each on a salad plate. Drain pineapple reserving ⅓ cup syrup. Drain crabmeat. Peel avocados; slice and arrange on lettuce slices. Top each with 2 slices of pineapple and the crabmeat. Combine reserved pineapple syrup, vinegar, olive oil, garlic salt, mustard and tarragon in a small jar. Shake well to blend. Stir in capers and spoon over salad to serve. Makes 5 servings.

DOUBLE STRAWBERRY CROWN

A layered favorite that combines the classic combination of cheese and fruit in a tangy new way.

1 can (1 lb., 4 oz.) Dole Pineapple Chunks
1 package (6 oz.) strawberry gelatin
1½ cups boiling water
1 cup halved fresh strawberries
1 cup dairy sour cream
2 ounces bleu cheese, crumbled

Drain pineapple reserving all syrup. Dissolve gelatin in boiling water. Stir in pineapple syrup. Chill mixture until thickened enough to hold shape in a spoon. Be sure pineapple is well drained. Combine with strawberries and one cup of gelatin. Turn into a deep 2-quart mold. Chill firm. Blend sour cream, bleu cheese and remaining gelatin. Turn into mold over fruit layer. Chill firm. Makes 8 servings.

TANGY COTTAGE CHEESE RING

A winning cottage cheese salad with lots of tang the entire family will like.

1 package (6 oz.) lemon gelatin
2 cups boiling water
1 can (1 lb., 4 oz.) Dole Crushed Pineapple
1 tablespoon vinegar
2 teaspoons seasoned salt
1 cup dairy sour cream
1 cup cottage cheese
1 tablespoon chopped parsley
1 tablespoon snipped chives

Dissolve gelatin in boiling water. Drain pineapple to make 1 cup syrup. Add to gelatin with vinegar and seasoned salt. Chill until mixture reaches consistency of unbeaten egg white. Fold in pineapple, sour cream, cottage cheese, parsley and chives. Turn into a 2-quart ring mold. Chill firm. Makes 8 to 10 servings.

Imperial Crab Salad

seafoam salad

A pale green froth of delicate flavor.

1 can (1 lb., 4 oz.) Dole Crushed Pineapple
1 package (6 oz.) lime gelatin
1 cup water
½ teaspoon seasoned salt
½ teaspoon dill weed
½ cup dry vermouth
2 cups dairy sour cream
Crisp salad greens

Drain pineapple well reserving all syrup. Add syrup to gelatin in a 2-quart saucepan. Stir in water, seasoned salt and dill weed. Heat mixture to boiling, stirring constantly to dissolve gelatin. Remove from heat. Stir in vermouth. Chill until mixture reaches consistency of unbeaten egg white. Blend in sour cream. Fold in pineapple. Pour into a 1½-quart ring mold. Chill firm. Unmold onto crisp salad greens to serve. Makes 6 to 8 servings.

zinging hot slaw

Pick up lagging winter appetites with this zippy cabbage slaw.

1 can (1 lb., 4 oz.) Dole Pineapple Chunks
6 slices bacon, diced
⅔ cup chopped onion
1 teaspoon flour
¼ cup vinegar
1 teaspoon salt
1 teaspoon dry mustard
½ teaspoon celery seed
4 cups finely shredded cabbage
⅓ cup diced green pepper

Drain pineapple reserving syrup. Cut bacon in ¼-inch slices and cook until crisp. Remove bacon with a slotted spoon and drain on paper towels. Discard all but 1 tablespoon fat from skillet, and sauté onion in the reserved fat until soft and transparent. Stir in flour. Add ¼ cup of the reserved pineapple syrup, vinegar, salt, mustard and celery seed. Cook, stirring, until mixture boils; keep warm. Combine cabbage, drained pineapple chunks and green pepper in salad bowl. Garnish with a tablespoon of the bacon. Add remaining bacon to hot dressing. Just before serving pour over salad and toss until well blended; serve at once. Makes 6 servings.

grandma's frozen salad

An old-fashioned favorite for a special treat.

1 can (1 lb., 4 oz.) Dole Crushed Pineapple
2 cups miniature marshmallows
1 package (8 oz.) cream cheese, softened
½ cup mayonnaise
½ teaspoon prepared mustard
1 cup whipping cream, whipped
6 drops red food coloring
2 cups sliced bananas (2 medium-large)
¼ cup chopped candied ginger
½ cup quartered maraschino cherries

Combine pineapple and all syrup with marshmallows; let stand 3 to 4 hours, until most of syrup is absorbed. Blend softened cream cheese with mayonnaise and mustard; fold in stiffly beaten cream. Blend in food coloring. Add pineapple-marshmallow mixture, bananas, ginger and cherries. Turn into 2-quart ring mold and freeze until firm. Cut into slices to serve. Makes 8 to 10 servings. *Note:* Mixture may be frozen in loaf pans or cans, if desired.

RUBY BORSCHT SALAD

Brimming with flavor, this salad is especially nice for a buffet—and happily, men love it!

1 can (1 lb., 4 oz.) Dole Crushed Pineapple
1 package (6 oz.) wild raspberry gelatin
1½ cups boiling water
1 can (1 lb.) shoestring beets
3 tablespoons plain vinegar
1 teaspoon dill weed
Dash salt
1 cup chopped celery
Dairy sour cream

Drain pineapple reserving all syrup. Dissolve gelatin in boiling water. Stir in beets and all liquid, vinegar, dill, salt and reserved pineapple syrup. Chill until mixture reaches consistency of unbeaten egg white. Fold in celery and pineapple. Pour into 2-quart mold. Chill firm. Top with sour cream and a sprinkle of dill weed to serve. Makes 8 servings.

CELEBRATION SALAD

This fresh tasting molded salad makes any dinner a celebration.

1 can (1 lb., 4 oz.) Dole Pineapple Chunks
1 can (16 oz.) pitted dark sweet cherries
2 packages (3 oz. ea.) black cherry gelatin
2 cups boiling water
2 tablespoons dry sherry
1 teaspoon grated lemon peel
2 tablespoons lemon juice
¼ teaspoon salt
⅛ teaspoon nutmeg
½ cup chopped pecans
Crisp salad greens
Dairy sour cream

Drain pineapple and cherries reserving all syrup. Dissolve gelatin in boling water. Stir in reserved pineapple and cherry syrup. Add sherry, lemon peel and juice, salt and nutmeg. Chill until mixture reaches consistency of unbeaten egg white. Fold in pineapple chunks, cherries and pecans. Pour into a 1½-quart mold. Chill firm. Unmold onto crisp salad greens. Serve topped with sour cream. Makes 6 to 8 servings.

TUNA POLYNESIAN

Quick as a wink, that's how easily this salad goes together. It's perfect for a busy-day lunch.

1 can (1 lb., 4 oz.) Dole Pineapple Chunks
2 cans (7 oz. ea.) solid packed tuna
1 cup diagonally sliced celery
1 tablespoon instant minced onion
¼ cup mayonnaise
¼ cup dairy sour cream
1 teaspoon curry powder
1 teaspoon seasoned salt
Crisp salad greens

Drain pineapple reserving 2 tablespoons syrup. Drain tuna well. Chunk tuna; combine with pineapple in a deep bowl. Add celery. Allow onions to stand in reserved pineapple syrup until rehydrated. Blend mayonnaise, sour cream, curry powder and seasoned salt. Stir in onion. Pour over tuna tossing to combine. Spoon onto crisp salad greens to serve. Makes 4 to 6 servings.

Ruby Borscht Salad

ENTRÉES

DEVILLED SHORT RIBS

Meaty short ribs baked in a tangy mustard sauce are a favorite with men. They love to pick up the bones!

3½ lbs. Prime short ribs
1 can (1 lb., 4 oz.) Dole Pineapple Chunks
¼ cup Dijon-style mustard
2 tablespoons soy sauce
1 teaspoon thyme, crushed
¼ teaspoon garlic powder
¼ cup dry sherry
1 tablespoon cornstarch
¼ cup chopped green onions

Have butcher cut short ribs into serving-size pieces. Place fat side up in shallow roasting pan. Drain pineapple reserving all syrup. Blend ½ cup of pineapple syrup, mustard, soy sauce, thyme and garlic powder. Pour over ribs. Bake in 350°F. oven 2½ hours or until tender. Remove to heated serving platter. Blend remaining pineapple syrup, sherry and cornstarch. Stir into pan juices until thickened and clear. Stir in pineapple chunks and onions until heated through. Spoon over short ribs to serve. Makes 6 servings.

PINEAPPLE-PLUM GLAZED PORK

The subtle flavors of the Orient blend to make a superb glaze-like sauce.

6 large pork chops
2 teaspoons seasoned salt
¼ teaspoon powdered ginger
1 can (1 lb., 4 oz.) Dole Sliced Pineapple
½ cup plum jam
¼ cup chopped green onions

Snip a piece of fat from pork chops and render in skillet. Brown chops well on both sides. Sprinkle with seasoned salt and ginger. Drain pineapple reserving all syrup. Blend syrup and jam. Pour over pork chops. Cover and simmer 30 minutes. Remove cover; add pineapple slices and green onions. Spoon pan juices over to heat pineapple. Makes 6 servings.

SAVORY STUFFED SPARERIBS

Easy to prepare, these ribs are a nice change from the usual barbecued type—with a flavorful, moist stuffing.

2 racks spareribs (approx. 4½ lbs.)
6 slices bacon
1 cup chopped celery
1 can (1 lb., 4 oz.) Dole Crushed Pineapple
½ cup chopped green onions
1 tablespoon summer savory
½ teaspoon sage
2 teaspoons seasoned salt
1 package (8 oz.) cornbread stuffing mix
1 egg, lightly beaten

Wipe spareribs; place one rack in large roasting pan. Fry bacon until crisp; remove with slotted spoon, drain and crumble. Sauté celery in bacon drippings until it turns bright green. Remove from heat; blend in pineapple and all syrup, onions, summer savory, sage and 1 teaspoon seasoned salt. Add to cornbread stuffing mix. Add egg and toss well to combine. Stir in reserved bacon. Spread over spareribs; top with second rack of ribs. Sprinkle with 1 teaspoon of seasoned salt. Cover tightly with foil. Roast in a 450°F. oven 1 hour. Uncover pan, turn heat down to 400°F. and continue roasting 1½ hours longer. Makes 6 servings.

OVEN GLAZED CORNED BEEF

An attractive way to serve corned beef that takes it out of the ordinary boiled-dinner category.

5 lb. corned beef brisket
1½ tablespoons pickling spice
1 can (15¼ oz.) Dole Crushed Pineapple
1 cup brown sugar, firmly packed
1 tablespoon prepared horseradish
Dash salt

Place beef in a large kettle and cover with water. Add pickling spice, cover and simmer two hours. Remove from water and place in shallow roasting pan.* Drain pineapple well. Combine with brown sugar, horseradish and salt. Spoon over corned beef. Glaze in a 350°F. oven 30 minutes. Serve warm or chilled. Makes 10 servings.
*May be prepared to this point early in the day and refrigerated until ready to glaze. In this case increase oven cooking time 10 minutes.

ZESTY SAUSAGE LOAF

Sausage adds flavor and texture with the added zip of horseradish and barbecue sauce.

1 lb. ground sausage
2 lbs. ground chuck
1 can (13¼ oz.) Dole Crushed Pineapple
½ cup fine dry bread crumbs
½ cup smokey barbecue sauce
¼ cup instant minced onion
2 tablespoons chopped parsley
1 egg
2 teaspoons prepared horseradish
½ teaspoon garlic powder

Combine sausage and ground chuck until thoroughly mixed. Blend in pineapple and all syrup, bread crumbs, barbecue sauce, onions, parsley, egg, horseradish and garlic powder. Form into a loaf in a 9 x 12-inch glass baking pan. Bake in a 350°F. oven 1½ hours. Makes 6 to 8 servings.

25

SESAME TERIYAKI

Steaks take on new interest with skillful seasoning. Use sirloin in place of rib eye if you like.

4 rib eye steaks*
1 can (1 lb., 4 oz.) Dole Sliced Pineapple
¼ cup soy sauce
¼ cup dry sherry
2 tablespoons honey
1 teaspoon grated orange peel
½ teaspoon ground ginger
¼ teaspoon garlic powder
1 tablespoon cornstarch
1 tablespoon toasted sesame seeds

Score fat edges of steaks if needed. Place in large flat glass baking dish. Drain pineapple reserving ¾ cup syrup. Combine syrup, soy sauce, sherry, honey, orange peel, ginger and garlic powder in a small jar. Shake well to blend. Pour over steaks. Marinate 2 to 3 hours turning occasionally. Remove steaks from marinade and place on rack in broiling pan. Broil 4 to 5 inches from heat, 8 minutes on first side. Turn steaks, arrange pineapple slices around steaks on pan. Brush all well with marinade. Broil 4 minutes for rare. Meanwhile, pour marinade into small saucepan. Stir in cornstarch. Heat to boiling, stirring constantly until mixture thickens. Remove steaks to heated serving platter; arrange pineapple slices over top. Pour pan juices into thickened marinade. Spoon over steaks. Sprinkle with toasted sesame seeds to serve. Makes 4 servings.
*Or filet mignon

SALMON STEAKS RÉMOULADE

Salmon steaks—fresh or frozen—are a real treat when topped with tangy herbed sauce.

4 salmon steaks (¾-inch thick)
Salt and pepper to taste
1 tablespoon soft butter
¼ cup syrup from pineapple
¼ cup dry white wine
1 tablespoon lemon juice
Rémoulade Sauce

Sprinkle salmon steaks with salt and pepper. Arrange on broiler pan and brush lightly with butter. Combine remaining ingredients. Broil fish, 6 inches from heat, about 5 minutes on each side. Baste with wine mixture occasionally. Serve at once with Rémoulade Sauce. Makes 4 servings.

RÉMOULADE SAUCE

¾ cup mayonnaise
1 tablespoon Dijon-style mustard
1½ tablespoons chopped chives
1½ tablespoons chopped green onion
1½ tablespoons chopped parsley
1½ tablespoons capers, chopped lightly
1 tablespoon tarragon wine vinegar
¾ teaspoon dried tarragon, crumbled
1 can (8¼ oz.) Dole Crushed Pineapple

Combine mayonnaise with mustard, chives, onion, parsley, capers, vinegar and tarragon. Drain pineapple well reserving ¼ cup syrup for salmon baste. Mix drained pineapple into mayonnaise. Chill thoroughly before serving to blend flavors. Makes about 1⅓ cups.

VIENNESE PORK CHOPS

Pork cooked the Austrian way brims with flavor and tenderness. Sour cream is a typically delicious touch.

6 large pork chops
1 can (1 lb., 4 oz.) Dole Crushed Pineapple
1 jar (32 oz.) sauerkraut
½ cup chopped green onions
1 teaspoon caraway seeds
2 teaspoons seasoned salt
¼ teaspoon garlic powder
Dairy sour cream

Cut a bit of fat from pork chops; render in a large skillet. Brown chops well. Drain pineapple. Combine with undrained sauerkraut, onions and caraway seeds. Pour into bottom of a deep 3-quart casserole. Arrange pork chops over top. Sprinkle with seasoned salt and garlic powder. Cover and bake in a 350°F. oven 1 hour. Serve topped with sour cream. Makes 6 servings.

OXTAILS CREOLE

Simmered slowly in a spicy broth, this rich, flavorful meat makes a delicious stew.

6 lbs. oxtails (cut into 2-inch pieces)
2 tablespoons butter
1 tablespoon seasoned salt
2 teaspoons chili powder
2 teaspoons dry mustard
1 can (1 lb., 4 oz.) Dole Pineapple Chunks
2 tablespoons lemon juice
1 teaspoon Worcestershire sauce
½ cup raisins
1 can (4 oz.) pimientos
2 cups chunked celery
1 cup halved pitted ripe olives
2 tablespoons cornstarch
2 tablespoons water
Hot cooked rice

Sauté oxtails in butter in a heavy 4-quart Dutch oven until well browned. Sprinkle with seasoned salt, chili powder and mustard. Drain pineapple reserving all syrup. Add syrup to oxtails along with lemon juice and Worcestershire sauce. Cover and simmer 1 hour. Skim excess fat from pan. Add raisins and cook 1 hour longer. Drain and cut pimientos into strips. Add to oxtails along with pineapple, celery and olives. Cover and simmer 30 minutes. Stir cornstarch into water; stir into stew until thickened. Serve over hot rice. Makes 6 to 8 servings.

chicken marrakesh

Exotic flavors of the Arab world create a savory succulent chicken so tender it falls off the bones!

5 lbs. frying chicken, cut up
¼ cup butter
2 tablespoons olive oil
2 tablespoons chopped fresh parsley
1 teaspoon salt
1 teaspoon summer savory
½ teaspoon garlic powder
½ teaspoon coarsely ground black pepper
⅛ teaspoon cayenne pepper
⅛ teaspoon powdered saffron
1 large onion, thinly sliced
1 lemon cut into 8 wedges
½ cup stuffed green olives
1 can (1 lb., 4 oz.) Dole Pineapple Chunks

Sauté chicken in butter and olive oil in a heavy Dutch oven. Sprinkle with parsley, salt, summer savory, garlic powder, black pepper, cayenne pepper and saffron, turning chicken pieces to coat. Add onion and lemon wedges. Turn heat to simmer; cover and cook very slowly 1½ hours. Remove chicken pieces to heated serving platter (chicken will be *very* well cooked). Halve olives lengthwise; drain pineapple chunks. Stir into pan juices until heated through. Pour over chicken to serve. Makes 4 to 6 servings.

della robbia pot roast

Wreathed in fruit and simmered in a rich herb-seasoned sauce, it's fit for the most discriminating guests.

1 tablespoon butter
5 lb. blade chuck roast
2 teaspoons garlic salt
½ cup brandy
1 can (1 lb., 4 oz.) Dole Sliced Pineapple
1 teaspoon beef stock base*
2 teaspoons fines herbes
10 large prunes
½ cup dried apricots
1 tablespoon cornstarch
2 tablespoons water
½ cup walnut halves
½ cup chopped green onions

Melt butter in a Dutch oven. Brown roast well on both sides. Sprinkle with garlic salt during browning. Remove from heat. Add brandy and ignite, spooning liquid over roast until flame dies. Drain pineapple reserving all syrup. Add syrup to roast along with beef stock base. Sprinkle with fines herbes. Add prunes and apricots. Cover tightly and simmer 2 to 2½ hours until tender. Blend cornstarch into water. Stir into pan juices until thickened. Add pineapple slices, walnuts and green onions spooning gravy over to heat. Makes 6 servings.
*Or use one beef bouillon cube.

Chicken Marrakesh

CROWN OF LAMB ROYALE

A spectacular entrée for very special guests. The baste on the meat adds both flavor and glaze.

6 lb. crown roast of lamb
1 can (1 lb., 4 oz.) Dole Pineapple Chunks
2 tablespoons butter
1 cup raw regular rice
½ teaspoon curry powder
1 tablespoon chicken seasoned stock base
2 teaspoons garlic salt
½ teaspoon dried mint leaves, crumbled
⅛ teaspoon nutmeg
1 cup peeled diced tomatoes
½ cup chopped green onions

Place lamb in a large shallow roasting pan. Wad a piece of foil and place in center cavity. Roast in a 325°F. oven 2½ hours. Meanwhile drain pineapple well reserving ¼ cup syrup for baste. Add water to remaining syrup to make 2 cups liquid. Melt butter in a 2-quart saucepan; stir in rice until coated. Stir in curry powder until foamy. Add liquid, chicken stock base, garlic salt, mint leaves and nutmeg. Cover and simmer 25 minutes or until all liquid is absorbed. Stir in pineapple chunks, tomatoes and onions just before serving. One half hour before roast is done, brush several times with baste to glaze. To serve, remove foil from center and place roast on large serving platter. Fill center with rice mixture. Makes 4 to 6 servings.
Baste: Combine reserved pineapple syrup with 2 tablespoons honey, ½ teaspoon dried mint leaves, crumbled and ½ teaspoon garlic salt. Blend well.

SWEET 'N SOUR COUNTRY RIBS

This moist heat method of oven cooking insures that ribs are tender and well done before being sauced, seasoned and browned.

3 to 3½ lbs. country-style spareribs
1 teaspoon salt
¾ cup water
¼ cup chopped onion
1 teaspoon oil
1 can (1 lb., 4 oz.) Dole Pineapple Chunks
½ cup catsup
¼ cup dry sherry
2 tablespoons brown sugar, firmly packed
2 tablespoons wine vinegar
2 tablespoons soy sauce
½ teaspoon powdered ginger
¼ teaspoon dry mustard
¼ teaspoon black pepper
Dash cayenne

Arrange spareribs in a large baking pan; sprinkle with salt. Add water. Cover with foil, bake in a 325°F. oven 1½ hours or until meat is tender. Meanwhile, sauté onion in oil. Drain pineapple reserving ¼ cup syrup. Combine reserved syrup with onion, catsup, and all remaining ingredients. Spoon over ribs; bake uncovered 30 minutes longer, basting occasionally. Add drained pineapple chunks last 5 minutes of baking. Makes 5 to 6 servings.

Crown of Lamb Royale

LEG OF LAMB AMSTERDAM

The flavor of good gin, blended with currant jelly and rosemary, sauces lamb to perfection.

6 lb. leg of lamb
1 can (1 lb., 4 oz.) Dole Crushed Pineapple
2 teaspoons salt
½ teaspoon dry mustard
¼ teaspoon garlic powder
½ teaspoon rosemary, crushed
½ cup red currant jelly
¼ cup gin
1½ tablespoons cornstarch

Place lamb fat side up in large roasting pan. Drain pineapple reserving all syrup. Combine 2 tablespoons syrup with salt, mustard, garlic powder and ¼ teaspoon rosemary. Spoon over lamb. Roast in 325°F. oven 2 hours for medium (2½ hours for well done). Remove lamb to heated serving platter. Remove excess fat from pan. Stir currant jelly, gin, remaining pineapple syrup, ¼ teaspoon rosemary and cornstarch into pan juices, scraping bottom of pan to dissolve browned bits. Cook stirring constantly until mixture boils and thickens. Stir in pineapple. Serve over lamb. Makes 6 to 8 servings.

BEEF STEW BRAZILIA

A delightfully different stew full-bodied enough for the most hungry group.

2 lbs. stewing beef
2 tablespoons butter
1 can (1 lb., 4 oz.) Dole Pineapple Chunks
1 can (1 lb.) whole tomatoes
1 cup water
1 tablespoon seasoned salt
½ bay leaf
½ teaspoon black pepper
½ teaspoon garlic powder
1 teaspoon oregano
4 small yellow onions
1 large sweet potato
1 large green bell pepper

Brown beef very well in butter in a heavy 2-quart saucepot. Drain pineapple reserving all syrup. Add syrup to beef with tomatoes and water. Stir in seasoned salt, bay leaf, pepper, garlic powder and oregano. Peel and quarter onions. Pare and slice sweet potato. Add onions and sweet potato to beef. Cover and simmer 1½ to 2 hours until meat is tender. Remove seeds from pepper and cut into chunks. Add to stew with pineapple chunks. Cook 10 minutes longer. Makes 6 to 8 servings.

PRAWNS BENGAL

Delicately seasoned, this prawn dish gets added flavor from the cucumbers and leeks.

2 lbs. fresh or frozen prawns
2 tablespoons butter
2 teaspoons chili powder
½ teaspoon curry powder
2 teaspoons garlic salt
1 large cucumber, peeled and diced
1 large leek, sliced
1 can (1 lb., 4 oz.) Dole Pineapple Chunks, drained
1 tablespoon lemon juice
Hot buttered rice
Moist flaked coconut

Shell and clean prawns. Melt butter in large skillet. Stir in chili and curry powder until frothy. Sauté prawns over medium heat until they turn pink. Sprinkle with garlic salt during cooking. Add cucumber to prawns with leeks cooking until leeks begin to wilt. Stir in pineapple chunks and lemon juice tossing to heat through. Serve over hot buttered rice topped with flaked coconut. Makes 4 to 6 servings.

Prawns Bengal

cornish hens continental

A small party for special friends is the perfect time to serve Cornish hens.

4 Cornish game hens (about 1 lb., 4 oz. ea.)
1 teaspoon salt
¼ teaspoon pepper
¼ teaspoon basil, crushed
1 tablespoon soft butter
1 can (13¼ oz.) Dole Crushed Pineapple
1 teaspoon cornstarch
⅛ teaspoon dry mustard
⅛ teaspoon dill weed
1 teaspoon soy sauce
1 teaspoon catsup
1 teaspoon wine vinegar
Continental Rice

Thaw Cornish hens, if frozen. Remove giblets. Combine salt, pepper and basil, and rub over body cavities of hens. Tie legs and place in shallow roasting pan. Rub skins with butter. Bake in a 400°F. oven 40 minutes until browned and almost tender. Meanwhile drain pineapple reserving all syrup; set aside ½ cup drained crushed pineapple for rice. Return remaining drained pineapple to the syrup; add cornstarch, mustard, dill, soy sauce, catsup and wine vinegar. Heat to boiling, stirring constantly. Spoon thickened pineapple mixture over Cornish hens. Bake 10 to 15 minutes longer until nicely glazed. Spoon Continental Rice onto serving platter. Place Cornish hens on top to serve. Makes 4 servings.

Continental Rice: Use ½ cup dry white wine and water to make volume of liquid required for 1 package (6 oz.) White and Wild Rice Mix. Add 2 tablespoons butter and contents of seasoning envelope and heat to boiling. Stir in rice from package and the reserved ½ cup crushed pineapple; bring back to a boil. Cover, turn heat low and cook 15 minutes. Add ¼ cup sliced almonds; stir lightly with a fork. Allow to stand, covered, in a warm place for 5 minutes before serving.

lamb chops melbourne

Delicately herbed lamb chops are moist and juicy cooked this way.

6 large round-bone lamb chops
1 tablespoon butter
2 teaspoons garlic salt
1 can (1 lb., 4 oz.) Dole Sliced Pineapple
2 teaspoons dried mint leaves
¼ teaspoon rosemary
¼ teaspoon black pepper
¼ cup dry sherry
1 tablespoon cornstarch

Brown lamb chops in butter in a large skillet. Sprinkle with garlic salt during browning. Drain pineapple reserving all syrup. Pour ½ cup syrup over chops. Sprinkle mint, rosemary and pepper over all. Add sherry. Cover and simmer 30 minutes. Remove chops to heated serving plate. Remove excess fat from pan. Blend cornstarch into remaining pineapple syrup. Cook stirring constantly until mixture boils and thickens. Add pineapple slices and heat through. Spoon over lamb chops to serve. Makes 6 servings.

POACHED SOLE PAGO PAGO

Beautifully glazed and seasoned, nutritious sole has special appeal for waistline watchers.

1 lb. filet of sole (4 small filets)
1 tablespoon butter
¼ cup dry white wine
¼ cup soy sauce
2 tablespoons lemon juice*
1 can (13¼ oz.) Dole Pineapple Chunks
3 tablespoons chopped green onion
½ teaspoon cornstarch

Fold filets in halves. Melt butter in large skillet. Arrange sole in single layer in butter. Combine wine, soy sauce and lemon juice; pour over fish, and heat to boiling. Turn heat low, cover pan and simmer 5 minutes. Meanwhile, drain pineapple well. Turn filets over and place pineapple chunks on top. Sprinkle with green onion. Cover pan and cook 2 to 3 minutes longer. Remove fish to heated serving platter and keep warm. Stir cornstarch into a teaspoon pineapple syrup or water and blend into pan juices. Cook, stirring constantly, until sauce boils and thickens. Spoon over fish and pineapple and serve at once. Makes 4 servings.
*Or use white wine vinegar

PORK CHOPS BAR LE DUC

The French touch of vermouth with cassis is used here, making pork chops a company best entrée!

6 large pork chops
2 teaspoons garlic salt
1 can (1 lb., 4 oz.) Dole Sliced Pineapple
½ cup black currant jam
1 teaspoon thyme
½ cup dry vermouth
⅓ cup crème de cassis
1½ tablespoons cornstarch
¼ cup chopped green onions

Snip a piece of fat from pork chops. Render in a large skillet. Sauté chops until brown. Sprinkle with garlic salt during browning. Drain pineapple reserving all syrup. Blend ½ cup reserved pineapple syrup and black currant jam. Pour over chops. Sprinkle with thyme. Add vermouth and crème de cassis. Cover lightly and simmer 35 minutes. Remove chops to heated serving platter. Stir cornstarch into remaining pineapple syrup. Stir into pan juices. Cook over high heat stirring constantly until mixture boils and thickens. Add pineapple slices and spoon over chops. Sprinkle with green onions. Makes 6 servings.

peking pineapple ham

Crunchy celery, juicy pineapple and a blend of plum jam and ginger turn ham into a delicious Oriental dish.

2 cups cooked ham strips
2 tablespoons butter
1 can (1 lb., 4 oz.) Dole Pineapple Chunks
½ cup plum jam
¼ teaspoon ground ginger
1 cup sliced celery
¼ cup chopped green onions
Hot cooked rice

Sauté ham in butter until lightly browned. Drain pineapple reserving ¼ cup syrup. Add pineapple syrup and plum jam to skillet; blend well. Sprinkle with ginger. Cook until mixture coats and glazes ham. Stir in pineapple chunks, celery and onions tossing until heated through. Serve over hot cooked rice. Makes 4 servings.

COLOR-PASSION CURRY

Tomatoes give this curry a richer color than most. Mild and typical of the dishes from Northern India.

4 slices bacon
2 lbs. boneless lamb stew meat
1 tablespoon curry powder*
1 can (1 lb., 12 oz.) whole tomatoes
1 can (1 lb., 4 oz.) Dole Pineapple Chunks
1 tablespoon instant minced onion
2 teaspoons salt
½ teaspoon garlic powder
2 tablespoons cornstarch
½ cup water

Cut bacon into small pieces. Fry in a heavy 2-quart saucepot until crisp. Add lamb cubes and sauté until golden. Stir in curry powder until foamy. Add tomatoes. Drain pineapple reserving all syrup. Add syrup to lamb with minced onions, salt and garlic powder. Cover and simmer 2 hours. Blend cornstarch into water. Stir into curry mixture. Add pineapple chunks. Stir until mixture thickens and boils. Makes 6 servings.
*If milder curry is preferred, use 1½ to 2 teaspoons.

ham skillet romanoff

A meal in a skillet that goes together in a minute—it's colorful and tasty with sour cream and dill.

2 cups cooked ham chunks
2 tablespoons butter
1 can (1 lb., 4 oz.) Dole Pineapple Chunks
1 can (1 lb.) cut green beans, drained
1 teaspoon dill weed
1 cup halved cherry tomatoes
1 cup dairy sour cream

Sauté ham in butter until lightly browned. Drain pineapple reserving ¼ cup syrup. Add syrup to ham along with pineapple chunks and beans. Sprinkle with dill weed. Simmer 3 to 4 minutes until heated. Stir in tomatoes. Top with sour cream to serve. Makes 4 servings.

Peking Pineapple Ham

kooftah kabobs

Kooftahs or meatball curries are favored in Central India. This variation puts the seasonings in the meat.

1 can (1 lb., 4 oz.) Dole Sliced Pineapple
2 lbs. ground chuck
½ cup fine dry bread crumbs
3 tablespoons soy sauce
2 tablespoons instant minced onion
2 teaspoons garlic salt
1 teaspoon curry powder
½ teaspoon ground cumin
1 large green bell pepper

Drain pineapple well reserving all syrup. Add pineapple syrup to ground chuck along with bread crumbs, soy sauce, onion, garlic salt, curry and cumin. Mix well. Form into 15 meatballs. Cut green pepper, remove seeds and cut into 15 chunks. On each of 5 long skewers thread a piece of green pepper, a meatball, a slice of pineapple, a meatball, and repeat ending with a pepper chunk. Grill 12 minutes on first side; turn and grill 8 minutes longer. Makes 5 generous servings.

california bean bake

If you don't have left-over ham strips, use sliced frankfurters instead. It's perfect for a hurry-up supper.

1 can (1 lb., 4 oz.) Dole Crushed Pineapple
2 cups cooked ham strips
2 tablespoons butter
1 can (1 lb., 12 oz.) baked beans
½ cup hickory smoked barbecue sauce
1 large green bell pepper, chunked
¼ cup chopped green onions

Drain pineapple well. Sauté ham strips in butter in an oven-proof skillet until lightly browned. Combine beans, barbecue sauce, green pepper, onions and pineapple. Stir into skillet. Bake in a 350°F. oven 20 minutes until flavors are blended and beans bubbly. Makes 4 servings.

brandied chicken livers

The delicate flavor of brandy permeates this colorful dish—perfect for a buffet or a Sunday brunch.

2 lbs. chicken livers
1 cup all-purpose flour
4 teaspoons garlic salt
½ teaspoon thyme
6 tablespoons butter
⅓ cup brandy
1 can (1 lb., 4 oz.) Dole Pineapple Chunks
1 cup halved cherry tomatoes
½ cup chopped green onions
Hot buttered rice

Pat chicken livers on paper towels to remove excess moisture. Combine flour, garlic salt and thyme in a plastic bag. Add chicken livers shaking well to coat. Sauté chicken livers in butter in a large skillet until browned and cooked through. Stir in brandy. Drain pineapple chunks well; add to the chicken livers with tomatoes and onions, tossing to heat through. Spoon onto hot buttered rice to serve. Makes 6 servings.

Kooftah Kabobs

tahitian chicken

Treat guests to a feast—for the eye as well as the palate—with this scrumptious Polynesian platter.

5 lbs. frying chicken, cut up
2 tablespoons butter
1 can (1 lb., 4 oz.) Dole Pineapple Chunks
¼ cup dry sherry
3 tablespoons soy sauce
¼ teaspoon garlic powder
2 teaspoons seasoned salt
2 tablespoons finely chopped crystallized ginger*
1 medium green bell pepper, chunked
1 jar (1 lb.) papaya chunks**
1 cup halved cherry tomatoes
½ cup chopped green onions
2 tablespoons cornstarch
2 tablespoons water

Sauté chicken in butter until well browned. Remove excess fat from pan. Drain pineapple reserving all syrup. Combine syrup with sherry, soy sauce and garlic powder. Pour over chicken. Sprinkle with seasoned salt and ginger. Cover and simmer 30 minutes. Remove chicken to a heated serving platter. Add green pepper, pineapple, papaya, cherry tomatoes and green onions to pan juices. Stir cornstarch into water; add to pan juices stirring gently until mixture thickens and boils. Spoon over chicken. Makes 6 servings.

*Or use 1 teaspoon ground ginger.
**Or use 1 fresh papaya, chunked.

Tahitian Chicken

Lamb shanks stofado

Lamb shanks cooked slowly in a rich fruit and herb sauce capture the aromatic flavors of Mediterranean cooking.

6 large lamb shanks
2 teaspoons seasoned salt
1 can (1 lb., 4 oz.) Dole Sliced Pineapple
2 cans (1 lb. ea.) whole unpeeled apricots
1 can (16 oz.) tomato sauce
1 teaspoon rosemary
1 teaspoon oregano
1 teaspoon dried mint leaves, crumbled
2 tablespoons cornstarch
¼ cup dry vermouth
1 cup walnut halves
2 tablespoons chopped chives

Have butcher crack bone in lamb shanks. Arrange in large roasting pan. Sprinkle with seasoned salt and roast in 450°F. oven 1 hour until browned. Drain pineapple and apricots reserving all syrup. Combine fruit syrup, tomato sauce, rosemary, oregano and mint. Pour over lamb. Place a piece of foil lightly over roasting pan, but do not tuck edges under. Turn heat to 350°F. and bake 1 hour longer until tender. Remove lamb shanks to heated serving platter. Blend cornstarch into vermouth. Stir into pan juices. Cook over medium heat until mixture boils and thickens. Stir in pineapple, apricots and walnuts until heated through. Pour over lamb shanks to serve. Garnish with chopped chives. Makes 6 servings.

Lamb Shanks Stofado

VEGETAbLES

BUffEt VEGEtAbLE RING

Delicate in flavor and dramatic, a party vegetable that goes together with very little fuss.

1 can (1 lb., 4 oz.) Dole Pineapple Chunks
3 tablespoons butter
1 cup raw regular rice
1 cup water
2 teaspoons garlic salt
2 teaspoons onion powder
1 chicken bouillon cube
½ teaspoon dill weed
¼ teaspoon nutmeg
3 packages (10 oz. ea.) frozen chopped spinach, thawed
1 can (16 oz.) baby beets
2 tablespoons brown sugar

Drain pineapple reserving all syrup. Melt 2 tablespoons butter in a 2-quart saucepan. Stir in rice until coated. Add all pineapple syrup and water. Blend in garlic salt, onion powder, bouillon cube, dill weed and nutmeg. Bring to a boil; cover and simmer 25 minutes. Drain spinach well. When rice is cooked, fold in spinach with a fork. Pack into a lightly oiled 10-inch ring mold.* Bake in a 375°F. oven 10 minutes. Meanwhile, drain beets reserving liquid. Slice beets into bite-size pieces, return to liquid and heat through. Drain well. Toss with one tablespoon butter and brown sugar until coated. Stir in pineapple chunks. Remove ring mold from oven. Place serving plate over mold; invert and shake mold to loosen. Spoon beet mixture into center of ring to serve. Makes 10 to 12 servings.
*May be prepared to this point early in the day, refrigerated and baked just before serving. In this case, bake 5 minutes longer.

STuffed acorn squash

A new way to dress up a favorite vegetable. Bake it right along with the ham or roast.

2 large acorn squash
1 lb. ground sausage
1 can (15¼ oz.) Dole Crushed Pineapple
1 tablespoon chopped parsley
½ teaspoon thyme
¼ teaspoon garlic powder
½ cup chopped green onion
Freshly ground pepper

Cut squash in halves; remove seeds. Cover with salted water and parboil 15 minutes. Drain and place cut-side up in baking pan. Meanwhile sauté sausage until well browned. Stir in pineapple and all syrup, parsley, thyme, garlic powder and onion until blended. Sprinkle pepper over squash. Spoon sausage mixture into squash. Bake in 350°F. oven 25 minutes. Makes 4 servings.

green coconut rice

This unusual rice dish turns any menu into something special.

1 can (13¼ oz.) Dole Crushed Pineapple
Water
1 tablespoon chicken seasoned stock base*
1 teaspoon finely chopped crystallized ginger
½ teaspoon dry mustard
1 cup raw regular rice
½ cup flaked coconut
⅓ cup finely chopped parsley
⅓ cup finely chopped green onions
2 tablespoons butter

Drain pineapple reserving all syrup. Add water to syrup to make 2 cups liquid. Combine liquid with chicken stock base, ginger and mustard in a 2-quart saucepan. Heat to boiling. Stir in rice. Cover and simmer 20 minutes or until rice is tender and all liquid is absorbed. Stir in coconut, parsley, onions, butter and pineapple. Makes 4 to 6 servings.
*Or use 2 chicken bouillon cubes.

captain's cabbage

Vivid red cabbage and brilliant green leeks make a striking dish.

1 can (1 lb., 4 oz.) Dole Pineapple Chunks
1 large thinly sliced leek (1 cup slices)
4 tablespoons butter
1 quart coarsely chopped red cabbage
1 teaspoon seasoned salt
1 teaspoon dill weed
Dairy sour cream

Drain pineapple well. Sauté leeks in butter in a large skillet until wilted. Stir in cabbage tossing until cooked tender-crisp. Sprinkle with seasoned salt and dill weed during cooking. Add pineapple chunks tossing until heated through. Serve topped with sour cream. Makes 4 to 6 servings.

herbed vegetable medley

Subtly seasoned, this colorful vegetable perks up lagging winter appetites with ease.

1 can (1 lb., 4 oz.) Dole Pineapple Chunks
⅓ cup white wine vinegar
2 tablespoons salad oil
2 teaspoons seasoned salt
2 teaspoons instant minced onion
¼ teaspoon seasoned pepper
¼ teaspoon basil
2 cups pared carrots, sliced diagonally, ½-inch thick
2 cups (2-inch) celery sticks

Drain pineapple and heat ½ cup of the syrup with vinegar, oil, salt, onion, pepper and basil. Add carrots and cook, covered, 10 minutes. Add celery and cook 10 to 15 minutes longer or until vegetables are tender-crisp. Add drained pineapple. Serve hot or cover and chill several hours or overnight. Makes 6 servings.

brandied sweet potato bake

An excellent choice when you'd rather not have last minute fussing with the vegetables.

2 cans (1 lb., 13 oz. ea.) sweet potatoes
1 can (1 lb., 4 oz.) Dole Pineapple Chunks
½ cup walnut halves
2 tablespoons butter
1 cup brown sugar, firmly packed
¼ cup brandy
½ teaspoon cinnamon
¼ teaspoon nutmeg
¼ teaspoon salt

Drain sweet potatoes and spread out in a flat 2-quart casserole. Drain pineapple. Arrange chunks over sweet potatoes. Sprinkle walnut halves over all. Melt butter. Blend in brown sugar, brandy, cinnamon, nutmeg and salt. Pour over sweet potatoes. Bake uncovered in a 375°F. oven 30 minutes. Makes 6 to 8 servings.

bourbon baked beans

Subtly flavored baked beans that really taste "home-made"—perfect for Saturday night suppers.

1 can (1 lb., 4 oz.) Dole Sliced Pineapple
2 cans (1 lb., 12 oz. ea.) baked beans
½ cup brown sugar, firmly packed
⅓ cup bourbon
3 tablespoons instant minced onion
1 tablespoon instant coffee
½ teaspoon dry mustard
4 slices bacon

Drain pineapple reserving ⅓ cup syrup. Combine beans, pineapple syrup, brown sugar, bourbon, onion, coffee and mustard in a 9 x 12-inch glass baking dish or large casserole. Allow to stand at room temperature one hour. Arrange pineapple slices over top of beans. Place bacon strips over pineapple. Bake uncovered in a 375°F. oven 1½ hours until bacon is browned and beans are bubbly. Makes 8 to 10 servings.

Herbed Vegetable Medley

45

BROILED tomato TOWERS

Plump fall tomatoes make a dramatic addition to the meal when topped this way and quickly broiled.

5 large tomatoes
1 can (1 lb., 4 oz.) Dole Pineapple Chunks
1 cup shredded Cheddar cheese
½ cup chopped green onions
1 teaspoon curry powder*
¼ cup mayonnaise

Wash tomatoes and cut in half crosswise; place on a large cookie sheet, cut-side up. Drain pineapple chunks. Toss with cheese and onions. Blend curry powder and mayonnaise. Combine with pineapple mixture. Spoon onto tomato halves.** Broil about 5 inches from source of heat 2 to 3 minutes until cheese is melted and lightly browned. Makes 10 servings.
  *Or use 2 tablespoons chopped green chiles.
**May be prepared to this point early in the day and refrigerated until ready to broil.

PILAU BENGAL

Mellow in flavor and not a bit hot. The recipe can be doubled easily.

1 can (1 lb., 4 oz.) Dole Pineapple Chunks
2 tablespoons butter
1 cup raw regular rice
2 teaspoons curry powder
1 tablespoon chicken seasoned stock base*
2 teaspoons onion powder
¼ cup raisins
2 tablespoons chopped parsley
2 tablespoons toasted slivered almonds

Drain pineapple reserving all syrup. Melt butter in a 2-quart saucepan. Stir in rice until each kernel is well coated. Add curry powder stirring until blended. Add water to reserved pineapple syrup to make 2 cups liquid. Pour over rice. Stir in chicken stock base, onion powder and raisins. Bring to boil. Cover. Reduce heat to simmer and cook 25 minutes. Stir in pineapple chunks, parsley and almonds just before serving. Makes 6 servings.
*Or use one chicken bouillon cube.

ORIENTAL STIR-FRY

Oriental vegetables are a joy to taste—crisp-cooked, colorful and deliciously sauced in soy.

2 cups diagonally sliced celery (¼-inch thick)
1 cup sliced green onion (¾-inch long)
1 cup sliced green pepper
1 tablespoon oil
⅓ cup water, chicken or beef broth
2 tablespoons soy sauce
1 can (13¼ oz.) Dole Pineapple Chunks
1 teaspoon cornstarch
½ teaspoon vinegar
1 tomato cut into wedges*

Combine celery, onion and green pepper in skillet with oil. Stir-fry over moderate heat for 3 minutes. Add water and soy sauce; cover and cook 5 minutes. Meanwhile, drain pineapple. Mix cornstarch with a teaspoon pineapple syrup. After vegetables have steamed 5 minutes, uncover and stir in cornstarch mixture. Add vinegar, drained pineapple and tomato. Heat 1 minute uncovered, stirring gently. Serve at once. Makes 5 to 6 servings.
*Or use ¾ cup cherry tomatoes, halved.

Broiled Tomato Towers

cookies & breads

golden macadamia bread

No need to butter this one! It's a crunchy, nut-crusted, moist bread that keeps very well.

1½ cups Royal Hawaiian Macadamia Nuts
1 tablespoon butter for pan coat
1 tablespoon sugar
½ cup butter
¾ cup sugar
1 egg
1 teaspoon vanilla
½ teaspoon grated lemon peel
2½ cups sifted all-purpose flour
2 teaspoons baking powder
1 teaspoon salt
½ teaspoon soda
1 can (8¼ oz.) Dole Crushed Pineapple
¼ cup milk

Chop macadamia nuts. Butter a 9 x 5 x 3-inch pan, using 1 tablespoon butter. Sprinkle with ¼ cup of the macadamia nuts, then with 1 tablespoon sugar. Cream ½ cup butter, ¾ cup sugar, egg, vanilla and lemon peel together until fluffy. Sift flour with baking powder, salt and soda. Blend into creamed mixture by hand, alternately with undrained pineapple and milk, mixing only until all of flour is moistened. Stir in remaining macadamia nuts. Turn into prepared pan. Bake on lowest shelf of preheated 350°F. oven 1 hour to 1 hour 10 minutes or just until loaf tests done. Let stand in pan 10 minutes, then turn out onto wire rack to cool. Makes 1 large loaf.

cocoa pecan puffs

A good "cookie jar" cookie to keep on hand for nibbling.

1 cup butter, softened
1½ cups brown sugar, firmly packed
1 egg
1 can (8¼ oz.) Dole Crushed Pineapple
3½ cups sifted all-purpose flour
3 tablespoons unsweetened cocoa
1 teaspoon baking powder
1 teaspoon cinnamon
½ teaspoon salt
½ cup chopped pecans

Cream butter until light. Beat in sugar until fluffy. Beat in egg until well blended. Fold in pineapple and all syrup. Combine flour, cocoa, baking powder, cinnamon and salt. Stir into pineapple mixture. Fold in pecans. Drop by teaspoonsful onto lightly greased cookie sheets. Bake in a preheated 375°F. oven 12 to 15 minutes or until lightly browned around edges. Remove to racks to cool before storing. Makes 4 to 4½ dozen cookies.

GOLDEN MERINGUE DESSERT BARS

The delicate meringue atop this three-layer bar makes it more like a dessert than a cookie.

Crust:
- ⅔ cup butter, softened
- ⅓ cup light brown sugar, firmly packed
- 2 egg yolks
- 1 teaspoon vanilla
- 1½ cups sifted all-purpose flour

Filling:
- 1 can (1 lb., 4 oz.) Dole Crushed Pineapple
- 1 cup dried apricots, cut up
- ½ cup sugar
- 3 tablespoons cornstarch
- 1 teaspoon grated orange peel
- ¼ teaspoon ground nutmeg

Orange Meringue:
- 3 egg whites
- ¼ teaspoon cream of tartar
- ⅔ cup sugar
- ½ teaspoon grated orange peel

Beat butter and brown sugar until light and fluffy. Beat in egg yolks and vanilla. Fold in flour until blended. Pat into a 9-inch square glass baking dish. Bake in a preheated 350°F. oven 15 minutes until lightly browned. Place on wire rack to cool. Meanwhile, drain pineapple reserving all syrup. Pour syrup over apricots in a small saucepan. Cook over medium heat, stirring occasionally for about ½ hour until all liquid is absorbed. Stir in sugar, pineapple, cornstarch, orange peel and nutmeg. Cook stirring constantly until mixture boils and becomes clear. (This will be very thick.) Remove from heat and cool slightly. Spread over crust. Beat egg whites to soft peaks. Add cream of tartar and beat in sugar gradually until stiff peaks form. Beat in orange peel. Spread over warm filling. Bake in a 350°F. oven 18 to 20 minutes until golden. Cool before cutting. Makes 16 bars.

Golden Meringue Dessert Bars

harvest gold muffins

Light and delicately sweet, with cake-like texture.

1 can (8¼ oz.) Dole Crushed Pineapple
2 cups sifted all-purpose flour
¼ cup sugar
1 tablespoon baking powder
¼ teaspoon salt
¼ teaspoon nutmeg
1 egg
1 cup milk
1 teaspoon grated orange peel
¼ cup melted butter

Drain pineapple very well pressing against sides of sieve to strain out moisture. Sift together flour, sugar, baking powder, salt and nutmeg. Beat together egg and milk; stir in pineapple and orange peel. Blend into dry ingredients by hand, along with butter, mixing as little as possible until all particles are moistened. Spoon into lightly greased 3-inch muffin pans. Bake in a preheated 400°F. oven 20 to 25 minutes until golden. Remove to wire rack to cool 5 minutes before removing from pan. Serve warm. Makes 1 dozen muffins.

pineapple dream bars

The sweet-tooth in the family will love these moist, rich, fruit and nut bars.

Crust: ½ cup soft butter
        ½ cup dark brown sugar, firmly packed
        1 cup sifted all-purpose flour

Filling: 1 can (13¼ oz.) Dole Crushed Pineapple
          2 eggs
          1 cup dark brown sugar, firmly packed
          5 tablespoons all-purpose flour
          1 teaspoon baking powder
          1 teaspoon cinnamon
          ¼ teaspoon salt
          ¼ teaspoon nutmeg
          1 teaspoon rum extract
          1½ cups flaked coconut
          1 cup coarsely chopped walnuts
          ½ cup halved maraschino cherries
          Sifted powdered sugar

Cream butter and brown sugar until well blended. Add flour, working with your hands until mixture is crumbly. Pat into bottom of a 13 x 9 x 2-inch pan. Bake in a preheated 350°F. oven 10 to 15 minutes until golden. Cool.

Drain pineapple well. Beat eggs with brown sugar until thick. Combine flour, baking powder, cinnamon, salt and nutmeg. Stir into egg mixture with rum extract. Fold in well drained pineapple, coconut, walnuts and cherries. Spread over crust. Bake in 350°F. oven 30 minutes until set. Cool slightly. Sprinkle with powdered sugar and cut into bars. Makes approximately 18 bars.

Harvest Gold Muffins

LunchBOX COOKIES

These are so easy to make the cookie jar need never be empty.

1 cup butter
1 cup sugar
2 eggs
3 cups sifted all-purpose flour
1 teaspoon soda
1 can (6 oz.) Dole Frozen Concentrated Pineapple Juice, thawed*
Cinnamon-sugar

Cream together the butter and sugar. Add eggs and beat until light and fluffy. Sift together flour and soda and add alternately to creamed mixture with ½ cup juice concentrate. Drop dough by teaspoonful 2 inches apart onto ungreased cookie sheets. Bake in a preheated 400°F. oven about 8 minutes or until lightly browned around edges. Brush hot cookies lightly with remaining concentrate; sprinkle with cinnamon-sugar. Remove cookies to cooling rack. Makes about 4 dozen small cookies.
*Or use Frozen Concentrated Pineapple-Orange Juice.

GLASGOW OAT BARS

Scottish oat cakes are famous for their deep, rich flavor.

1 can (1 lb., 4 oz.) Dole Crushed Pineapple
½ cup sugar
1 tablespoon cornstarch
Dash salt
1 tablespoon butter
2 teaspoons grated orange peel
Oat Crumbles

Pour pineapple into saucepan; boil rapidly for 10 minutes to reduce syrup. Blend sugar, cornstarch and salt well; stir into hot pineapple. Cook, stirring constantly until clear and thickened. Remove from heat, stir in butter and orange peel; cool. Prepare Oat Crumbles; spoon half into a 9 x 13 x 2-inch pan; pack down firmly. Cover evenly with pineapple mixture. Sprinkle remaining Oat Crumbles over top; press down lightly. Bake in a preheated 375°F. oven 20 to 25 minutes until lightly browned. Cool before cutting. Makes about 2½ dozen bars 1½ x 2-inches.

Oat Crumbles: Sift 2 cups all-purpose flour with 1 teaspoon baking powder and ½ teaspoon salt. Add 1½ cups brown sugar (firmly packed), 2 cups uncooked quick-cooking oats, and 1 cup butter; blend until crumbly.

GOLD MINE NUGGETS

Soft moist cookies that go together quickly.

½ cup shortening
¾ cup brown sugar, firmly packed
½ teaspoon vanilla
1 egg
1 can (8¼ oz.) Dole Crushed Pineapple
1 cup quick-cooking rolled oats
1 cup sifted all-purpose flour
1 teaspoon salt
½ teaspoon ground cinnamon
½ cup chopped walnuts
1 package (6 oz.) chocolate chips

Cream shortening, sugar and vanilla together until fluffy. Beat in egg and pineapple. Stir in remaining ingredients. Drop by teaspoonful on ungreased cookie sheets. Bake in a preheated 375°F. oven 15 to 17 minutes. Makes about 3 dozen cookies.

DESSERTS

SOUFFLÉ COINTREAU

Light and lovely soufflés are a spectacular dessert and fail safe, too, if the steps are followed exactly.

1 can (1 lb., 4 oz.) Dole Crushed Pineapple
2 tablespoons Cointreau
2 tablespoons cornstarch
¾ cup milk
1½ tablespoons butter
3 whole eggs
1 egg white
½ teaspoon cream of tartar
¼ teaspoon salt
¼ cup sugar
Sugar for top of soufflé
Cointreau sauce

Drain pineapple reserving all syrup. Combine 1 cup pineapple with Cointreau; warm gently. Butter a 5-cup soufflé dish. Fold a 25-inch length of foil 6-inches wide in half to make a 3-inch wide strip; fasten around top of dish, using a paper clip where foil overlaps. Secure with string around outside of dish so sides of dish are built up. Butter inside of collar. Stir cornstarch into milk in small saucepan; add butter. Heat to boiling over moderate heat, stirring until mixture thickens and comes to a full boil. Remove from heat. Separate whole eggs and beat yolks lightly. Slowly stir hot milk mixture into yolks. Beat the 4 egg whites with cream of tartar and salt until stiff. Gradually beat in sugar, beating to a stiff meringue. Fold about ¼ of the meringue into egg yolk mixture thoroughly; add remaining meringue and fold in quickly. Turn warm crushed pineapple and Cointreau into prepared dish. Spoon soufflé mixture into dish. Sprinkle top lightly with sugar. Set dish in shallow pan with about 1-inch hot water. Bake on lowest shelf of preheated 375°F. oven 30 minutes; turn heat down to 350°F. and bake about 20 minutes longer until set. Remove collar carefully and serve at once from soufflé dish. Makes 6 to 8 servings.

Cointreau Sauce: Stir 2 teaspoons cornstarch into reserved crushed pineapple and syrup; add 1 tablespoon dark corn syrup, 1 tablespoon butter, and a dash of salt. Heat to boiling, stirring constantly. Remove from heat and stir in ⅓ cup Cointreau. Serve warm. Makes 1½ cups sauce.

PINK GRAPEFRUIT BAVARIAN

Make this delicate creamy dessert in your prettiest tall mold the day before you plan to serve it.

1 can (46 oz.) Dole Pineapple-Pink Grapefruit Juice Drink
3 envelopes unflavored gelatin
1 cup whipping cream
½ cup sugar
Raspberry Rum Sauce

Sprinkle gelatin over two cups pineapple-pink grapefruit juice in saucepan. Let stand a few minutes to soften. Heat to boiling, stirring to dissolve gelatin. Add all remaining juice stirring well. Chill until mixture reaches consistency of unbeaten egg white. Whip cream with sugar until stiff. Fold into gelatin mixture. Pour into 6-cup mold. Chill firm overnight. Unmold and serve with Raspberry Rum Sauce. Makes 8 to 10 servings.

RASPBERRY RUM SAUCE

1 pkg. (10 oz.) frozen raspberries, thawed
1 cup water
1 tablespoon cornstarch
½ cup sugar
½ teaspoon pumpkin pie spice
¼ cup rum

Combine raspberries, water, cornstarch, sugar and pumpkin pie spice in a small saucepan. Heat until mixture boils and thickens. Remove from heat; stir in rum. Chill. Serve cold over Pink Grapefruit Bavarian. Makes approximately 1½ cups sauce.

OLD FASHIONED UPSIDE-DOWN CAKE

Just the way Grandma used to make it—rich with the addition of sour cream and beautifully sugar glazed.

⅔ cup butter
⅔ cup brown sugar, firmly packed
1 can (1 lb., 4 oz.) Dole Sliced Pineapple
9 maraschino cherries
2 eggs, separated
¾ cup granulated sugar
1 teaspoon grated lemon peel
1 teaspoon lemon juice
1 teaspoon vanilla
1½ cups sifted cake flour
1¾ teaspoons baking powder
¾ teaspoon salt
½ cup dairy sour cream

Melt ⅓ cup butter in 10-inch skillet with oven-proof handle. Add brown sugar and stir until well blended. Drain pineapple well reserving 2 tablespoons of syrup. Arrange slices close together in butter-sugar mixture. Extra slices may be cut into wedges and placed between slices. Center each whole slice with a cherry. Beat egg whites to soft peaks. Gradually beat in ¼ cup granulated sugar to make a stiff meringue. With same beater, beat remaining ⅓ cup butter with remaining ½ cup sugar until fluffy. Beat in egg yolks, lemon peel and juice, and vanilla. Sift flour with baking powder and salt. Blend into creamed mixture alternately with sour cream and 2 tablespoons pineapple syrup. Fold in egg white mixture. Pour over pineapple in skillet. Bake in a preheated 350°F. oven about 35 minutes until cake tests done. Let stand 10 minutes, then invert onto serving plate. Allow skillet to rest over cake a minute for syrup to drain. Serve warm or cold. Makes 8 servings.

Soufflé Cointreau, page 53

mai tai pie

Cool and light, the flavors of lime and rum are distinctive in this coconut crust pie.

2 cups flaked coconut
¼ cup butter, melted
1 can (1 lb., 4 oz.) Dole Crushed Pineapple
Water
2 envelopes unflavored gelatin
½ cup sugar
½ teaspoon salt
1 teaspoon grated lime peel
1 tablespoon lime juice
3 eggs, separated
½ cup dark Jamaican rum
2 tablespoons Cointreau
1 cup whipping cream
Twisted lime slices
Stemmed maraschino cherries

Combine coconut and melted butter, tossing with a fork to combine. Press over bottom and up sides of 9-inch glass pie plate. Bake in a preheated 300°F. oven 25 minutes until well browned. Cool.

Meanwhile, drain pineapple well reserving all syrup. Add water to syrup to make 1½ cups liquid. Sprinkle gelatin over liquid in a small saucepan. Stir in sugar, salt, lime peel and juice. Heat mixture to boiling, stirring constantly until sugar is dissolved. Remove from heat. Beat egg yolks until foamy. Gradually pour hot mixture over eggs, beating constantly. Stir in rum and Cointreau. Chill mixture about 40 minutes to consistency of unbeaten egg white. Beat egg whites until stiff peaks form. Fold into gelatin mixture until well blended. Whip cream until stiff. Fold cream and pineapple into gelatin mixture. Turn into pie shell. Chill two hours before cutting. Garnish with twisted lime slices and cherries to serve. Makes 1 (9-inch) pie.

soufflé amor frio

And "Cold Love" it is! A marvelous tasting fluff of fruit, cream and Grand Marnier.

1 can (13¼ oz.) Dole Crushed Pineapple
1 envelope unflavored gelatin
4 eggs, separated
⅓ cup Grand Marnier
¼ teaspoon salt
⅓ cup sugar
1 cup whipping cream

Turn pineapple and all syrup into top of double boiler; sprinkle gelatin over surface. Let stand a few minutes to soften gelatin, then set over boiling water. Beat egg yolks lightly and stir into pineapple. Cook, stirring constantly, until mixture coats spoon and gelatin is completely dissolved. Remove from heat and cool. Stir in Grand Marnier. Cool until mixture begins to thicken. Beat egg whites with salt to soft peaks. Gradually beat in sugar, beating to a stiff meringue. With same beater, whip cream stiff. Fold meringue and cream into gelatin mixture. Turn into a 6-cup soufflé dish; chill until firm. Makes 6 to 8 servings.

NOTE: Soufflé is too delicate to mold. Elegant made in after-dinner coffee cups, with waxed paper or foil collars, removing collars before serving.

Mai Tai Pie

pacific ginger torte

Had you heard tortes were difficult to make? Not so with this one—just refrigerate until ready to serve.

1 can (1 lb., 4 oz.) Dole Crushed Pineapple
1 package (14½ oz.) gingerbread mix
½ cup dairy sour cream
1 large banana, sliced
2 tablespoons lemon juice
1 cup whipping cream
¼ cup powdered sugar
1 teaspoon vanilla
½ cup chopped walnuts

Drain pineapple reserving ½ cup syrup. Blend reserved pineapple syrup into gingerbread mix. Beat in sour cream. Pour into two greased 8-inch round cake pans. Bake in a preheated oven 350°F. 20 to 25 minutes until it tests done. Turn out onto wire racks to cool. Meanwhile slice banana into lemon juice and toss to coat each slice well. Whip cream with sugar and vanilla until stiff. Place one layer gingerbread on serving plate. Spread with half whipped cream. Arrange banana slices around edge. Spoon half of drained pineapple into center. Top with remaining gingerbread layer. Spread with remaining whipped cream. Ring edge with walnuts, spoon remaining pineapple into center. Makes 8 to 10 servings.

castilian coconut cake

When winter's drear catches up to you, make this gay-as-a-daffodil cake to brighten your spirits.

1 can (8¼ oz.) Dole Crushed Pineapple
1 package (1 lb., 2½ oz.) yellow cake mix
¾ cup sugar
⅓ cup light corn syrup
¼ cup water
3 egg whites
Dash salt
1 teaspoon vanilla
½ cup flaked coconut

Drain pineapple well reserving all syrup. Mix cake batter according to package directions, using pineapple syrup for part of the liquid. Fold crushed pineapple into batter. Spoon into two greased and floured 9-inch layer cake pans. Bake in a preheated 350°F. oven 25 to 30 minutes until cake tests done. Let stand 10 minutes; turn out onto wire racks to cool. Combine sugar, corn syrup and water in small saucepan, and stir over moderate heat until sugar is dissolved. Boil to 242°F. on candy thermometer. (Syrup will spin an 8-inch thread when dropped from tip of spoon.) Beat egg whites with salt until stiff. Gradually beat in hot syrup, beating until mixture is thick enough to hold its shape. Beat in vanilla. Spread between layers and on top and sides of cake. Sprinkle with coconut, patting some against sides. Let stand until set before cutting. Makes 1 (9-inch) cake.

Pacific Ginger Torte

pineapple chiffon cake

Cloud light in texture and delicate in flavor, serve it plain or with ice cream or sherbet.

2¼ cups sifted all-purpose flour
1½ cups sugar
1 tablespoon baking powder
1 teaspoon salt
½ cup salad oil
7 egg yolks, unbeaten
1 can (8¼ oz.) Dole Crushed Pineapple
1 teaspoon grated lemon peel
1 tablespoon lemon juice
2 tablespoons water
2 teaspoons vanilla
1 cup egg whites (7 or 8)
½ teaspoon cream of tartar

Sift flour with 1 cup sugar, baking powder and salt into mixing bowl. Make a "well" in center of dry ingredients and add oil, egg yolks, pineapple with all syrup, lemon peel and juice, water and vanilla. Beat until mixture is well blended. Beat egg whites with cream of tartar in a large mixing bowl to soft peaks. Slowly beat in remaining ½ cup sugar, continuing to beat to very stiff meringue. Pour pineapple mixture slowly over entire surface of egg whites, gently cutting and folding in with rubber spatula until completely blended. Turn into an ungreased 10-inch tube pan. Bake on lowest rack in a preheated 325°F. oven 65 to 70 minutes until cake tests done. Invert pan and let hang until cold. Makes 1 large cake (approx. 16 servings).

mile high pineapple pie

Topped with a mountain of meringue, this classic pineapple pie has a light delicate flavor.

1 can (1 lb., 4 oz.) Dole Crushed Pineapple
1½ cups sugar
½ cup water
⅓ cup cornstarch
¼ cup dry sherry
2 teaspoons grated lemon peel
¼ teaspoon salt
4 eggs, separated
2 tablespoons butter
9-inch baked pastry shell
¼ teaspoon cream of tartar

Combine pineapple with all syrup, 1 cup sugar, water, cornstarch, sherry, lemon peel and salt in a saucepan. Stir well to combine. Heat to boiling, stirring constantly until mixture boils and thickens enough so that spoon leaves path when drawn through mixture. Remove from heat. Beat a little hot mixture into egg yolks. Return to hot mixture and cook, stirring constantly, 1 minute longer. Stir in butter and pour at once into pastry shell. Beat egg whites with cream of tartar until soft peaks form. Beat in ½ cup sugar, gradually adding 2 tablespoons at a time until very stiff peaks form. Spread over warm filling, sealing to edge of crust. Bake in a preheated 400°F. oven 7 to 10 minutes or until golden. Cool on wire rack 1 hour before serving. Makes 1 (9-inch) pie.

PINEAPPLE POTS DE CRÈME

Rich and silken is the texture of this cloud-light dessert. It melts in your mouth!

4 extra-large egg yolks
½ cup sugar
Dash salt
3 tablespoons dark Jamaican rum
2 packages (8 oz. ea.) cream cheese, softened
1 can (8¼ oz.) Dole Crushed Pineapple
1 teaspoon grated lemon peel
1 cup whipping cream
Semi-sweet chocolate curls

Beat egg yolks with sugar, salt and rum until thick and creamy. Add cheese and beat until smooth and light. Drain pineapple very well. Fold into cheese mixture with lemon peel. Whip cream until stiff. Fold into cheese mixture. Spoon into 12 pot de crème cups or stemmed sherbets. Chill 2 hours or more. Just before serving, sprinkle with chocolate curls. Makes 12 servings.

FRUIT CUP KASHMIR

A good, tart fruit cup with fresh flavor that gives a nice light touch to a fall or winter menu.

1 can (1 lb., 4 oz.) Dole Pineapple Chunks
1 can (11 oz.) mandarin oranges
½ cup sliced dates
1 red apple
1 fresh pear
1 banana
2 tablespoons honey
1 teaspoon grated lime peel
2 tablespoons lime juice
Toasted coconut

Drain pineapple, reserving ½ cup syrup. Drain oranges. Combine pineapple, oranges, and dates in a deep glass bowl. Core apple and pear, leaving skins on. Cut into bite size chunks. Slice banana. Toss apple, pear and banana with pineapple. Blend honey, lime peel and juice into reserved pineapple syrup. Pour over fruit, tossing lightly. Chill well. Serve topped with toasted coconut. Makes 6 to 8 servings.

AMBROSIAL CHEESELESS CHEESE TARTS

Creamy rich filling that tastes almost like cheesecake is the basis for these elegant tarts.

1 can (1 lb., 4 oz.) Dole Pineapple Chunks
1 package (3¾ oz.) instant French vanilla pudding mix
1 cup dairy sour cream
6 (3-inch) baked pastry tart shells
1 cup orange marmalade
2 teaspoons cornstarch
¼ cup flaked coconut

Drain pineapple well reserving ½ cup syrup. Combine instant pudding mix and sour cream until blended. Beat in reserved pineapple syrup until well blended and mixture thickens slightly. Spoon into tart shells. Chill 20 minutes. Heat orange marmalade with cornstarch to boiling; cool until thickened. Top tarts with pineapple chunks. Spoon marmalade over to glaze and sprinkle coconut over all. Chill 2 hours before serving. Makes 6 (3-inch) tarts.

PRESERVES

PRESTO PINEAPPLE JELLY

Tart-sweet with the tang of lime, this easy-do jelly is reminiscent of fine English breakfast marmalade.

1 lime
1 can (6 oz.) Dole Frozen Concentrated Pineapple Juice
1 can (6 oz.) Dole Frozen Concentrated
   Pineapple-Grapefruit Juice*
1 package (1¾ oz.) dry pectin
2½ cups water
5½ cups sugar
½ teaspoon ground ginger
Hot paraffin wax

Using a potato peeler, pare lime peel very thinly being sure not to get any white underskin. Cut lime peel into very thin 1-inch slivers. Squeeze juice and reserve. Combine pineapple juice concentrate and pineapple-grapefruit juice concentrate with pectin and water in a large saucepan. Stir constantly over high heat until bubbles form around the edge. Add sugar, ginger, lime peel and juice all at once. Bring to a full rolling boil. Boil hard one minute, stirring constantly. Remove from heat, skim. Pour into 8 sterilized jelly jars. Cover at once with hot paraffin. Makes 8 (8 oz.) jars.
*Or use Frozen Concentrated Pineapple-Orange Juice.

chunky PINEAPPLE chutney

Simple and easy to make, the chunky pieces of pineapple give this chutney an interesting texture.

3 cans (1 lb., 4 oz. ea.) Dole Pineapple Chunks
4 cups dark brown sugar, firmly packed
3 cups cider vinegar
2 whole cloves garlic
1 package (15 oz.) raisins
1 package (11 oz.) currants
1 lb. broken walnut pieces
3 tablespoons chopped crystallized ginger
2 tablespoons instant minced onion
1 tablespoon grated orange peel
1½ teaspoons salt
1 teaspoon ground allspice
1 teaspoon ground cinnamon
½ teaspoon pepper
½ teaspoon ground nutmeg

Combine pineapple and all syrup with remaining ingredients in a large kettle. Bring to boil; boil over medium heat one hour until thick. Pour into sterilized jars and cover. (There is no need to seal with paraffin). Makes 3 quarts.

Chunkey Pineapple Chutney
Pineapple Apricot Conserve, *page 64*
Tipsy Chutney, *page 64*

QUICK SPICED PINEAPPLE

Delicately spicy, this easy-do condiment is the perfect accompaniment to a cold buffet.

1 can (1 lb., 4 oz.) Dole Pineapple Chunks
⅔ cup sugar
⅓ cup wine vinegar
Dash of salt
1 teaspoon whole cloves
½ teaspoon whole allspice
2 sticks cinnamon

Drain pineapple reserving ¾ cup syrup. Combine syrup with remaining ingredients. Heat to a full rolling boil; reduce heat and boil gently for 10 minutes stirring occasionally. Pour hot syrup over pineapple. Cover and cool slowly. When cool, chill for several hours or overnight in refrigerator. Can be stored in refrigerator up to 2 weeks. Makes 8 to 10 servings.

TIPSY CHUTNEY

Spicy and rich, this crunchy chutney has the definite tang of lime. It's especially nice served with lamb.

3 cans (1 lb., 4 oz. ea.) Dole Crushed Pineapple
4 large limes
2 cups red wine vinegar
1 box (1 lb.) dark brown sugar
2 cups light raisins
2 cups dark raisins
1 cup dark Jamaican rum
1 cup coarsely chopped pecans
¼ cup chopped crystallized ginger
3 tablespoons instant minced onion
1½ teaspoons salt
1 teaspoon ground nutmeg
1 teaspoon ground allspice
1 teaspoon ground cinnamon
¼ teaspoon garlic powder

Turn pineapple and all syrup into a large open kettle. Wash and cut limes into quarters, leaving peels on. Combine limes and wine vinegar in blender jar. Whir until chopped. Add to pineapple along with all remaining ingredients. Bring to rolling boil. Cook uncovered over medium heat one hour until thick. Remove and pour into sterilized jars. Cool; cover and refrigerate. (There is no need to seal with paraffin.) Makes approximately 2 quarts.

PINEAPPLE-APRICOT CONSERVE

Perfect for gift giving—make this conserve in pretty containers to use as a hostess gift.

1 pound dried apricots
1½ cups water
3 medium-size oranges
1 can (1 lb., 4 oz.) Dole Crushed Pineapple
3 cups sugar

Combine apricots with water. Simmer, uncovered about 15 minutes or until apricots are soft and most of water is absorbed. Grate 3 tablespoons peel from oranges. Peel oranges, removing all of white membrane. Cut fruit in sixths and remove seeds. Combine apricots and orange pieces in blender and purée. Turn into large kettle; add undrained pineapple, orange peel and sugar. Simmer over low heat until thick, about 6 to 8 minutes, stirring frequently. Spoon into jars, cover closely, and refrigerate (or seal in sterilized jars). Makes about 1¾ quarts.

BEVERAGES

SPIRITED DUCK PUNCH

Simple to make, with good full-bodied flavor, wine fanciers enjoy this party punch.

1 can (6 oz.) Dole Frozen Concentrated Pineapple Juice
1 can (6 oz.) Dole Frozen Concentrated Pineapple-Orange Juice
1 cup brandy
1 bottle (one-fifth) Burgundy, chilled
1 tray ice cubes
1 bottle (one-fifth) Cold Duck

Combine pineapple juice and pineapple-orange juice concentrates, brandy and Burgundy in a large punch bowl. Add ice cubes and Cold Duck just before serving. Makes 16 (4 oz.) servings.

PUNCH BOWL OLD FASHIONEDS

Bourbon lovers enjoy this punch. It's full flavored and not too sweet.

1 can (6 oz.) Dole Frozen Concentrated Pineapple-Orange Juice
1 can (6 oz.) Dole Frozen Concentrated Pineapple-Grapefruit Juice
1 quart bourbon
1 jar (9 oz.) stemmed maraschino cherries
1 orange, thinly sliced
2 trays ice cubes
2 quarts ginger ale, chilled

In a large punch bowl combine pineapple-orange juice and pineapple-grapefruit juice concentrates with bourbon until thoroughly blended. Stir in cherries with all juice, orange slices and ice. Just before serving, stir in ginger ale. Makes approximately 25 (4 oz.) servings.

FRIDAY FRUIT SHAKE

Simple enough to let the children do themselves, this nutritious fruit shake uses ingredients at hand.

1 can (12 oz.) Dole Pineapple Juice
1 medium-size banana
Dash salt
1 pint vanilla ice cream

Combine all ingredients in blender. Whir smooth. Makes 3 cups.

PINK CHAMPAGNE PUNCH

Bubbling, pink and pretty, this is an excellent choice for an afternoon reception or evening buffet party.

1 can (46 oz.) Dole Pineapple-Pink Grapefruit Juice Drink
½ cup sugar
1 teaspoon Angostura bitters
½ cup brandy
1 bottle (one-fifth) pink champagne
Ice cubes

Have all ingredients well chilled. Combine pineapple-pink grapefruit juice drink, sugar, bitters and brandy in a large punch bowl. Add champagne and ice just before serving. Makes approximately 16 (4 oz.) servings.

fireside wine warmer

Warm and spicy, this is a perfect thirst-quencher on a cold winter evening. Serve in sturdy earthenware mugs.

1 can (46 oz.) Dole Pineapple-Pink Grapefruit Juice Drink
½ cup sugar
2 tablespoons butter
5 lemon slices
10 whole cloves
3 cinnamon sticks
½ large bottle burgundy (about 14 oz.)
Whipped cream, optional
Nutmeg, optional

Put pineapple-pink grapefruit juice drink, sugar, butter, lemon slices, cloves and cinnamon sticks into a large saucepan or kettle. Bring to a boil, then add burgundy, cover and simmer (do not boil) for 20 minutes. Serve in mugs. If desired, top with a dollop of sweetened whipped cream and a sprinkling of nutmeg. Makes about 15 (4 oz.) servings.

maui foam

Pale pink, smooth and creamy, this delicately flavored drink is a favorite with the ladies.

1 can (6 oz.) Dole Pineapple Juice
4 oz. light rum
2 oz. brandy
2 oz. whipping cream
4 ice cubes
2 oz. maraschino syrup

Combine all ingredients in blender. Whir one minute until smooth. Pour into three stemmed glasses. Makes 3 servings.

sunshine breakfast nog

Wonderful way to greet the day, this easy-do breakfast provides good nutrition in a glass.

1 can (6 oz.) Dole Frozen Concentrated Pineapple-Orange Juice
3 eggs
Nutmeg

Reconstitute pineapple-orange juice concentrate as directed with 3 cans of water. Shake well to blend. Combine 1 cup juice with 1 egg in blender. Blend until frothy. Top with nutmeg to serve. Repeat twice again. Makes 3 servings.
Note: If a sweeter nog is desired, add 1 tablespoon honey with each egg.

harvest festival shrub

An old English thirst-quenching treat, a "shrub" traditionally gets its tang from vinegar.

1 can (46 oz.) Dole Pineapple Juice
1 quart cranberry juice cocktail
1 can (12 oz.) apricot nectar
1 tray ice cubes
2 tablespoons cider vinegar
2 packages (10 oz. ea.) frozen raspberries
1 orange, sliced
1 lemon, sliced

Combine pineapple juice, cranberry juice cocktail and apricot nectar in a large punch bowl. Add ice cubes. Stir in cider vinegar and raspberries. Garnish with orange and lemon slices to serve. Makes 30 (4 oz.) servings.

holiday fare

holly BERRY salad WREath

A brilliant festive addition to any holiday buffet.

1 package (3 oz.) lime gelatin
1 package (3 oz.) strawberry gelatin
2 cups boiling water
2 cups cold water
Fresh parsley sprigs
3 maraschino cherries
1 can (13¼ oz.) Dole Crushed Pineapple, drained
1 cup whole cranberry sauce
2 tablespoons sliced almonds
Crisp salad greens
Dairy sour cream

In separate bowls, dissolve each flavor gelatin in one cup boiling water. Stir in one cup cold water. Pour ½ cup lime gelatin into bottom of a 1½-quart ring mold. Chill remaining lime gelatin and strawberry gelatin until syrupy.

Arrange parsley in gelatin in mold to form a wreath. Cut maraschino cherries into pieces to resemble holly berries. Arrange in parsley in gelatin. Chill until almost set.

Stir crushed pineapple into remaining thickened lime gelatin. Pour over parsley layer. Refrigerate.

Meanwhile, stir cranberries and almonds into thickened strawberry gelatin. Pour over pineapple layer. Chill until set. Unmold on serving plate. Garnish with crisp salad greens and serve with sour cream or mayonnaise. Makes 10 to 12 servings.

harvest festival turkey

A flavorful cornbread stuffed turkey for Thanksgiving.

12 lb. turkey
Salt
1 cup butter
½ cup slivered almonds
1 cup sliced celery
1 can (1 lb., 4 oz.) Dole Crushed Pineapple
1 cup chopped green onions
¼ cup dry sherry
2 teaspoons thyme
2 teaspoons grated orange peel
1 teaspoon garlic salt
1 package (13 oz.) crumb-style cornbread stuffing mix

Wipe turkey well. Lightly salt inner cavity. Melt butter in a large skillet. Sauté almonds until golden. Remove and reserve. Sauté celery until it turns bright green. Remove from heat; stir in pineapple and all syrup, onions, sherry, thyme, orange peel and garlic salt. Toss lightly with stuffing mix. Stir in almonds. Stuff cavity of turkey lightly and truss. Place in large open roasting pan. Roast in a 325°F. oven 3½ to 4 hours, basting with pan drippings occasionally. Place remainder of stuffing in lightly buttered casserole. Cover and bake the last 45 minutes of roasting time. Makes 8 servings.

stuffed edam cheese

A festive appetizer for the holidays.

1 Edam cheese (about 9 oz.)
1 package (3 oz.) cream cheese
2 oz. bleu cheese (¼ cup crumbled)
½ teaspoon seasoned salt
½ teaspoon caraway seed
¼ teaspoon dry mustard
2 drops tabasco
1 can (8¼ oz.) Dole Crushed Pineapple
2 tablespoons chopped parsley
1 tablespoon chopped pimiento

Allow cheese to stand out until softened. Cut top from Edam cheese in a cone; hollow out with a teaspoon. Beat removed cheese with cream and bleu cheeses. Blend in seasonings. Drain pineapple well; fold into cheese mixture, along with parsley and pimiento. Heap mixture into Edam shell. Garnish with a parsley sprig and a slice of pimiento. Makes about 2 cups spread.

scandinavian fruit salad

A delicate fruit salad with a surprise dressing.

1 can (1 lb., 4 oz.) Dole Pineapple Chunks
1 can (1 lb.) apricot halves
1 cup halved seeded grapes
1 large red apple
1 large banana
¼ cup orange Curacao
¼ cup light salad oil
2 tablespoons lemon juice
1 teaspoon dried mint leaves, crumbled
½ teaspoon anise seed, crushed
¼ teaspoon dry mustard
2 quarts crisp salad greens

Drain pineapple reserving ½ cup syrup. Drain apricots. Combine pineapple, apricots and grapes in a deep bowl. Core and chunk apple, leaving skin on; peel and slice banana; add to fruit. Combine reserved pineapple syrup, orange Curacao, oil, lemon juice, mint, anise seed and mustard until blended. Pour over fruit. Cover and chill at least 4 hours or overnight for flavors to blend. When ready to serve, toss with crisp greens. Makes 6 to 8 servings.

crunchy cranberry crown

Sparkle up the holiday table with this tart, crunchy salad.

1 can (1 lb., 4 oz.) Dole Crushed Pineapple
2 packages (3 oz. ea.) raspberry gelatin
2 cups boiling water
1 can (16 oz.) whole cranberry sauce
1 teaspoon grated lemon peel
3 tablespoons lemon juice
¼ teaspoon salt
1 cup sliced celery
½ cup chopped walnuts
Crisp salad greens

Drain pineapple reserving all syrup. Dissolve gelatin in boiling water. Stir in pineapple syrup, cranberry sauce, lemon peel and juice and salt. Cool until mixture reaches consistency of unbeaten egg white. Fold in pineapple, celery and nuts. Pour into a 1½-quart mold. Chill firm. Unmold onto crisp salad greens to serve. Makes 6 to 8 servings.

Holly Berry Salad Wreath, page 67

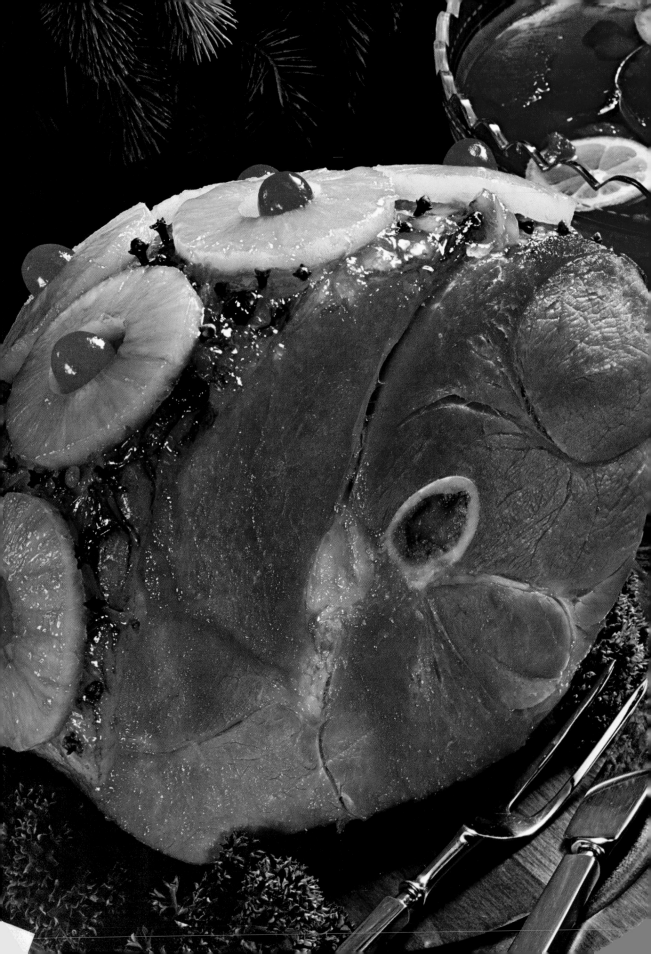

holiday Baked ham

Sparkle up the holiday table with this tangy glazed ham.

8½ lb. bone-in smoked ham
1 can (1 lb., 4 oz.) Dole Sliced Pineapple
1 cup apricot preserves
1 teaspoon dry mustard
½ teaspoon ground allspice
Whole cloves
Maraschino cherries

Remove rind from ham; place fat side up on rack in open roasting pan. Insert meat thermometer with bulb centered in thickest part of meat. Bake in a 325°F. oven until thermometer registers 140°F.* Meanwhile, drain pineapple reserving all syrup. Combine syrup with apricot preserves, mustard and allspice. Boil to reduce by half. Remove ham from oven ½ hour before done. Using toothpicks, skewer pineapple slices over entire ham surface. Stud with cloves. Toothpick a cherry into center of each pineapple slice. Brush with glaze and return to oven. Continue brushing with glaze every 10 minutes until done. Makes 8 to 10 servings.
*18-20 minutes per lb. for fully-cooked ham;
22-25 minutes per lb. for cook-before-eating ham.

Lion's Gate Punch

A hearty bowl for merry making. Particularly enjoyed by the men.

2 cans (6 oz. ea.) Dole Frozen Concentrated Pineapple Juice
1 can (6 oz.) pink lemonade frozen concentrate
2 cups rum
1½ cups cherry brandy
¼ cup grenadine
1 package (10 oz.) frozen raspberries
2 quarts soda water, chilled
1 bottle (one-fifth) pink champagne
Ice cubes

Combine frozen pineapple juice and lemonade concentrates in a large punch bowl. Stir in rum, cherry brandy and grenadine. Stir in frozen raspberries, soda and champagne. Add ice and serve. Makes approximately 36 (4 oz.) servings.

Roast duckling ananas

Duckling cooked this way is crispy-skinned and tasty.

5-lb. duckling
2½ teaspoons seasoned salt
1 can (1 lb., 4 oz.) Dole Crushed Pineapple
½ cup brandy
¼ cup crème de cassis
¼ teaspoon nutmeg
1 tablespoon cornstarch
2 tablespoons water

Cut duckling into quarters. Place on rack in roasting pan skin side down. Sprinkle with 2 teaspoons seasoned salt. Roast in a 350°F. oven one hour. Remove excess fat from pan. Turn duckling skin side up. Increase heat to 400°F. and roast 35 to 40 minutes until skin is well browned. Remove to heated serving platter. Skim excess fat from pan; add pineapple and all syrup, brandy and crème de cassis. Stir in nutmeg and ½ teaspoon seasoned salt. Blend cornstarch into water; stir into pineapple mixture, heating until thickened. Serve over duck. Makes 4 servings.

Overleaf:
Holiday Baked Ham
Lion's Gate Punch
Scandinavian Fruit Salad, *page 69*

72

noël eggnog

Rich and smooth, the fruit base keeps it from being too heavy.

6 eggs, separated
½ cup powdered sugar
¾ cup granulated sugar
1 cup dark rum
1 cup brandy
1 can (46 oz.) Dole Pineapple Juice
1 can (6 oz.) Dole Frozen Concentrated
    Pineapple-Orange Juice, thawed
1 quart whipping cream
Nutmeg

Beat egg whites with powdered sugar until light and fluffy. Using same beater, beat egg yolks until well whipped. Beat in sugar until thick and lemon-colored. Gradually beat in rum and brandy. Stir in pineapple juice and pineapple-orange juice concentrate. Pour over egg whites, folding to combine well. Stir in one pint cream. Whip remaining cream until stiff. Fold into pineapple mixture. Pour into large punch bowl. Sprinkle with nutmeg to serve. Makes 25 (4 oz.) servings.

viennese almond torte

So buttery-rich is this almond pastry that it melts in your mouth!

1 can (1 lb., 4 oz.) Dole Crushed Pineapple
2½ tablespoons arrowroot
⅔ cup sugar
⅛ teaspoon salt
¼ cup chopped maraschino cherries
½ cup almond paste
½ cup butter
2 tablespoons shortening
1 egg yolk
¼ teaspoon salt
1⅔ cups sifted all-purpose flour
1 tablespoon milk
Powdered sugar

Combine pineapple and all syrup with arrowroot. Cook over moderate heat, stirring frequently, until mixture boils and thickens. Remove from heat; stir in ⅓ cup sugar, salt and cherries. Cool. Cream together almond paste, butter and shortening. Add egg yolk, remaining ⅓ cup sugar and salt; blend well. Gradually blend in flour and milk to make a stiff dough. Shape into a ball and cut in thirds. Set aside ⅓ for lattice top. Press remainder over bottom and about ¾ inch up sides of a 9-inch layer cake pan. Spoon pineapple filling into pan. On lightly floured board, roll remaining dough to a rectangle, about 9 x 6-inches. Cut into narrow strips, and arrange lattice over pineapple filling, lifting strips carefully by sliding onto blade of long spatula (dough is rich and breaks easily). Press ends of strips against dough at sides of pan. Re-roll any trimmings, and cut short strips for edge of pan, pressing together lightly at seams. Bake in a preheated 375°F. oven 35 to 40 minutes, until pastry is browned. Cool. Sift powdered sugar lightly over torte to serve. Makes 1 (9-inch) torte.

Bouchée de Noël

Traditional in France for the Christmas feast.

⅓ cup sifted cake flour
¼ cup unsweetened cocoa
½ teaspoon baking powder
¼ teaspoon salt
4 eggs, separated
¾ cup sugar
1 teaspoon vanilla
Pineapple Crème Filling
Chocolate Glaze

Sift flour with cocoa, baking powder and salt. Beat egg whites until stiff. Gradually beat in sugar, beating to a stiff meringue. Beat egg yolks with vanilla until thick and light. Fold into egg whites. Gradually fold in flour mixture. Turn into greased 10 x 15 x 1-inch pan lined with waxed paper and greased again. Bake in a preheated 400°F. oven 10 to 13 minutes, until cake springs back when touched lightly in center. Turn out onto cloth covered with sifted powdered sugar. Strip off waxed paper; roll cake loosely. Cool on wire rack. When cold, unroll and remove cloth. Spread with Pineapple Crème Filling and re-roll. Place on serving plate. Spoon Chocolate Glaze along top of roll and spread with small spatula. Let stand until set before cutting. Makes 8 to 10 servings.

Pineapple Crème Filling

¼ cup sugar
3 tablespoons cornstarch
¼ teaspoon salt
1 can (1 lb., 4 oz.) Dole Crushed Pineapple
1 egg, beaten
½ cup whipping cream

Combine sugar, cornstarch and salt in saucepan; stir in undrained pineapple. Cook and stir over moderate heat until clear and thickened. Quickly stir in egg. Return to very low heat and cook a minute longer, stirring briskly. Cover and cool. Whip cream and fold into cooled pineapple mixture. Makes about 3¼ cups.

Chocolate Glaze

2 squares (1 oz. ea.) semi-sweet chocolate
2 tablespoons shortening
2 teaspoons light corn syrup

Melt chocolate with shortening over hot water. Stir in corn syrup. Use glaze at once.

Bouchée de Noël

CRATCHET'S CHRISTMAS PUDDING

As much a part of the British holiday celebration as the joy of the season. It comes to the table all aglow!

⅔ cup chopped suet
⅔ cup chopped candied orange peel
¼ cup chopped candied lemon peel
1½ cups raisins
1 cup chopped figs
2 cups graham cracker crumbs
1 cup sugar
1 tablespoon cinnamon
1 teaspoon salt
1½ teaspoons ginger
½ teaspoon allspice
¼ teaspoon nutmeg
1 can (8¼ oz.) Dole Crushed Pineapple
⅓ cup raspberry preserves
4 eggs
¾ cup brandy
Almond Cream Sauce

In a large bowl, combine suet, orange and lemon peels, raisins, figs, crumbs, sugar, cinnamon, salt and spices. Toss to combine. Blend pineapple and all syrup with raspberry preserves. Stir into fruit mixture. Beat eggs until foamy. Stir in ½ cup brandy. Fold into fruit until just blended. Turn into a well-greased 2-quart pudding mold or 9-cup Bundt pan. Cover tightly. (If Bundt pan is used, press foil firmly into outer edges and around center hole to cover completely.) Place on a rack in a large kettle. Pour boiling water into pan until it reaches halfway up mold. Cover and steam 4 hours. (Water should be gently boiling.) Remove from water. Cool 5 minutes. Invert on serving plate and remove mold. Heat ¼ cup brandy in a small saucepan over medium heat. Ignite with wooden match; pour over mold to serve. Serve with Almond Cream Sauce. Makes 12 servings.

ALMOND CREAM SAUCE

1 package (3¼ oz.) vanilla pudding mix (not instant)
½ teaspoon almond extract
1 cup whipping cream
1 cup milk
¼ cup brandy

Blend all ingredients except brandy in a small saucepan. Heat to boiling, stirring constantly. Remove from heat; stir in brandy. Serve warm or cover tightly and chill well. Beat in electric mixer until smooth and creamy before serving. Makes 2½ cups sauce.

Cratchet's Christmas Pudding

BRANDIED FRUIT WREATH

A spectacular cream puff fruit wreath—easy to make—that brings a holiday meal to a finish with flair!

½ cup butter
1 cup water
¼ teaspoon salt
1 cup sifted all-purpose flour
4 eggs
1 egg yolk
¼ cup sliced blanched almonds

Filling:
1 can (1 lb., 4 oz.) Dole Pineapple Chunks
1 can (11 oz.) mandarin oranges
½ cup halved maraschino cherries
2 bananas
¼ cup brandy
2 cups whipping cream
¾ cup sugar
1 tablespoon cornstarch
⅛ teaspoon mace

Combine butter, water and salt in a heavy 2-quart saucepan. Boil slowly until butter is melted. Remove from heat and immediately stir in all flour, beating to blend thoroughly. Return to heat, beating 1 to 2 minutes until mixture leaves sides of pan, forms a mass and begins to form film on bottom of pan. Remove from heat. Beat eggs into mixture one at a time until each is absorbed before adding next. When well blended, drop by dessert spoonsful onto a lightly greased cookie sheet. Place in a ring approximately 9 inches in diameter, allowing batter to touch to form a wreath. Bake in a preheated 425°F. oven 30 minutes or until puff has doubled in size and is lightly browned. Beat egg yolk lightly; brush over top of wreath. Sprinkle with almonds. Reduce heat to 375°F. and bake 10 minutes longer or until firm and crusty. With a long sharp knife, cut slits in sides of puff all around edge. Turn oven off and leave door ajar. Allow puff to remain in oven 10 minutes longer. Remove; carefully cut top off of puff. Scrape out any soft uncooked portions with a fork and cool. Slip lower part of puff onto large serving platter. Spoon filling into lower portion. Replace top of puff. Chill 1 hour before serving. Makes 12 servings.

Filling: While puff is baking, drain pineapple and oranges very well. Turn into small bowl with cherries and sliced bananas. Pour brandy over all, cover and marinate. When ready to assemble, whip cream with sugar, cornstarch and mace until stiff. Fold in fruit and brandy.

InDEX